Dean

enjoy being a

woman

with Respect

The
POWER
of a
WOMAN

The POWER *of a* WOMAN

Leading The Way

Anna Maria Clement, Ph.D., N.M.D., L.N.
Katherine C. Powell, Ed.D.

HIPP CRATES
HEALTH INSTITUTE

Library of Congress Cataloging-in-Publication Data

ISBN-13: 978-1-4675-8053-3 (Paperback)
ISBN-10: 1-4675-8053-8 (Paperback)

Publisher: Hippocrates Health Institute
        1443 Palmdale Court
        West Palm Beach, FL 33411

Cover design by Larissa Hise Henoch
Inside design and formatting by Lawna Patterson Oldfield

Contents

Acknowledgments

This book, a product of past and current research, is a collaborative and adventurous effort by the authors to provide: (1) a foundation of the history of female leadership; (2) strategies on how to remain healthy by balancing work and home; and, (3) tools drawn from actual experiences of many leaders gracious enough to share their knowledge.

We believe that women have always been powerful, either covertly or overtly, but now is the time for us to take the reins of leadership. The last 15 years have seen an abuse of power in the political and corporate sectors that has set us back in our efforts to reach prosperity. A series of leaders, almost universally male, scammed the American public by ignoring auditing protocols, removing (or flagrantly violating) SEC regulations, and basically embodying the attitude of *"take the money and run."* We believe that the future of our country, the global economy, and the survival of healthy people depend on authentic female leadership. We present our case here, in which we hope to make clear that there is no other choice for survival.

We would like to thank those who joined our team for this production, and are particularly grateful for the participation of our talented interviewees. The staff of Hippocrates Health Institute (HHI) has been incredible; without their support this book would not exist. We especially thank Darlene, Diane, Tarin, and Viviene, who support Drs. Brian and Anna Maria Clement. Of course, there are many others to thank—HHI is a super team. We also thank Health Communications, Inc., and the members of its publishing staff, who always seem to be giving 100% of their time, with smiles and creative ideas. We especially thank Dan, Larissa, Gina, Lawna, and Dawn; they complement each other and work together without missing a beat.

We would also like to thank our esteemed and unique editor, Josh Weinberger, whose editing talents are unsurpassed. Josh was on the staff of *The New Yorker* magazine and then traveled extensively around the world before starting his own consulting firm in New York City. We were fortunate to engage him in our project as he juggles parenting duties for his preschool twins, Timothy and Penelope, with their successful mom, Saskia, who works full time. We are grateful for his creative ideas, ability to see our vision, and expertise to make sure we got it right. We did this book together. His family-work balance is a great example for the future of our country.

We thank our friends and family who put up with our journey to provide the tools for future female leaders—and for *all* leaders who might learn from our book. We hope they enjoy it.

WE DEDICATE THIS BOOK to our female family members, colleagues, and friends, as well as to all those who come to Hippocrates Health Institute to search for answers and to discover their own formula. We thank all our readers, and hope this book helps them in their journeys.

Preface

"*There never will be complete
equality until women themselves help to
make laws to elect lawmakers.*"

"*The fact is, women are in chains,
and their servitude is all the more debasing
because they do not realize it.*"

"*It was we, the people, not we,
the white male citizens; nor yet we,
the male citizens; but we, the whole people,
who formed this Union.*"

—SUSAN B. ANTHONY,

AMERICAN LEADER OF WOMEN'S RIGHTS AND SUFFRAGE

The Battle for Female Equality

The purpose of this book is to educate and empower women, and to give them tools and inspiration (via shared experiences) to follow their dreams and be healthy in the process. Work, family, and self-interest involve a balancing act. We need guidelines to remember how to keep this a priority. Many great female leaders around the world have struck this balance, and we hope to cast a spotlight on their accomplishments.

As described in the Introduction, our formula is quite simple: **Leadership** equals *authenticity* plus *boundaries.* Imagine a five-thousand-year-old dolmen (a stone temple) with the top slab as *leadership*, the left-hand column as *authenticity,* and the right-hand column as *boundaries.* Great leadership emanates from leaders who are powerful and can guide their followers. American women, for example, finally got the right to vote in 1920, thanks to the courage and efforts of, among others, American suffragette Susan B. Anthony and her followers during the nineteenth century. Their manifesto on women's rights was based on the book *A Vindication of the Rights of Women* written by Mary Wollstonecraft in 1792. Her written words were warm, engaging, and full of passion. These women were swimming upstream yet they continued their fight for women's rights. Today we are still fighting for these rights.

Our book is divided into three major sections, with three parts in sections one and three, and four parts in section two:

Section One: **Women and Leadership**—depicting great female leaders, personality attributes, and their accomplishments from the beginning of western civilization until now.

Section Two: **Balancing the Divide**—describing major male/female differences, balancing them, and reviewing the principles of great leadership, as well as experiences from leaders .

Section Three: **Bridging the Divide**—balancing home and work by being healthy, using the differences to bridge the gap, and becoming great male/female leaders, as partners or teams.

Leaders are great when they embrace their authentic selves with clear boundaries and are open to growth and creativity. To capture leadership criteria and firsthand experiences, we interviewed several female and male leaders about their views on leadership. Those interviews appear throughout the book, providing an in-depth look at their various career experiences.

Women and Power

Historically, women have been the caretakers of the home and children. World War II changed opportunities for women. In the middle of the twentieth century, the powers that be recognized—or at least, were forced by circumstance to acknowledge—the proficiency and effectiveness of women in the workplace. Billie Jean King, for example, became a great leader, first in women's tennis and then in society as whole, challenging (and shattering) the stereotypical view of women. She helped change society's view of women's capabilities by beating Bobby Riggs in a 1973 tennis match viewed by millions worldwide. By that time, many women (with or without children) were totally dedicated to their careers; however, those who were mothers all agreed that the biggest challenge was balancing their work and home-life needs.

Women may have begun to achieve some status in sports but equal-rights laws didn't come to the forefront until 1970s. In corporate America, young women of the 1960s and 1970s wanted change and were willing to squash their instincts for perceived equality. Women wanted and still want equal pay. This aspect of the women's revolution, significantly fueled by corporate and business interests, resulted in the weakening of the nuclear family, and a burgeoning sense of loss among mature women who felt they were forced to sacrifice their opportunity to have children. Those who sought to "have it all" faced challenges. Of course, no one—women or men—should be judged for (or made to doubt) their choices, but instead encouraged to pursue what they love. Passion is one of the greatest attributes leaders must possess.

International studies often cite the countries of Scandinavia as three of the top five "happiest" nations. Even though modern Nordic cultures cherish harmony between the sexes, and have introduced commendable enhancements to women's status, there life is far from perfect. As long as little girls are led to believe that being pretty is more important than being happy, we will continue to see great disparities between men and women, and great obstacles to potential women leaders. Although feminine beauty is an asset, it should not be one's only power or defining characteristic. Beauty is within us, shining outward to enhance attraction and energy.

DR. ANNA MARIA CLEMENT: *Since I grew up in the country, I was always close to nature which gave me a realistic and practical attitude. I have always been connected to the land, the earth, and farming—eating natural foods for health. My dad and I have always shared health concerns and now I continue this process with Brian. We believe daily exercise and plant-based food are important health requirements. The brain, pain, compassion, and exercise are all interconnected and involve the hypothalamus (sleep, body temperature, activity governed by the pituitary gland). This is regulated by the release of GABA (gamma-aminobutyric acid), a neurotransmitter which transmits nerve impulses that help the body relax and reduce anxiety. My dad showed me how to handle responsibilities, reduce stress, and that work is a part of life, not who you are. As I continue my journey in the health field, I now share my passionate interests with Brian.*

As a young adult, I became dedicated to my passion for a healthy lifestyle. I could envision myself working with the latest discoveries. Another interest for me is the part of the brain called the "hippocampus" where memory, feelings and thinking interact and have an effect on health. This part of the brain is affected by how we feel and our thoughts. Feelings and emotions regulate so much of our health, as well as our reaction to pain and resistance to disease. How we think and act affects how we feel and how we get well. Now, as I am seeing so many women and men with various problems at the Hippocrates Health Institute, I understand more how the mind and body work together. I feel my dedication to my work originated from my wonderful family life and I continue to share what I know and learn.

As women see their roles continue to evolve, some have managed to raise children while becoming great leaders, not merely of local organizations and multinational corporations, but of entire countries. The secret is out: Women can do it. No one succeeds alone, of course, and successful women leaders depend on the help of both men and women—we are, for better or worse, in this world together. It is noted that African tribal nations had male leaders; however, when there was an emergency or life or death situations, they always elected a female leader to solve the problems quickly. Many countries do this currently.

Ours is the only major country in the world that has never had a female head of state. Even China once had a female empress. Several nations are currently led by women, such as Kosovo, Liberia, Lithuania, and South Korea. South America has several female presidents, such as Argentina, Chile, and Brazil. For example, Dilma Rousseff, president of Brazil since 2011, is leading her country toward economic and political success. She is well respected. Angela Merkel, the German chancellor since 2005, was involved in forming the European Union and was president of the European Council in 2007. Her work is considered to be of high regard in this past decade. She has great influence in the world economy. We believe there are many women of greatness who are more than capable of assuming leadership roles in America.

Women and Transformation

Women throughout history have been misshaping their very natures to fit societal expectations of their individual family or work lives. For generations, many women have seen themselves as power-less; since World War II they have slowly realized that they are strong and committed to do the work of men. Many countries counted on women during the war years to do the difficult jobs men once did—and women stepped up to do those jobs very well. Our victory, in the end, owed a great deal to the success of women who were occupying most of the jobs required in their country. Women were ready to take their proper place in the workforce.

After the war, as veterans returned home, most of these women were forcibly returned to roles as housewives. In the 1960s, the rela-tively few women who did enter the workforce had to adapt to male standards of behavior and dress. Any traits deemed *"too feminine"* were unacceptable; to achieve recognition from (and be trusted by) their male counterparts and superiors, they were expected to outperform men holding similar positions. Their authentic selves and boundaries were confused along with males being fearful or threatened that their jobs were being replaced with women. New authentic-selves for females had to evolve with clear boundaries to keep sexual discrimination from entering their work environment.

We are now in a different era. In this century, women such as, former Secretary of State Hillary Clinton, Senator Elizabeth Warren, and Facebook's Sheryl Sandberg have proven themselves capable of participating in the new corporate and political arenas to become great leaders. For example, Kirsten Gillibrand (senator from New York) wrote *Off the Sidelines: Raise Your Voice—Change the World* (2014). She advocates zero tolerance for sexual assaults (military and schools), and domestic abuse. Young women must have an awareness of their value within the world, and must maintain their confidence and self-respect. As long as women work together, they provide each other support to succeed in fulfilling their potential.

DR. KATHERINE POWELL: After I graduated college in the late 1960s, and entered the corporate world, I had to embrace the corporate style for women at that time: pantsuits and boots. I was careful not to gossip or to talk too much; I knew there was an eye out for such female weaknesses. My work ethic was unequaled—it had to be. I had no home life and work consumed me. As a result, my accomplishments were notable: I was promoted to manager after only a couple of years, and became just the second woman in a Fortune 500 company's Executive Manpower Orientation Program (a nine-month regimen designed to guide future top-level executives). Though I heard others refer to me as the "token woman" manager, I was in a technical field where few people were qualified. As a result, my rewards were equal to those received by men in comparable positions—car services, executive privileges, including an expense account for travel and entertainment; however, I wanted more meaning in my life.

By the early '80s, however, I was no longer a token but rather a veteran of an invading army of women. Not only had the uniform changed—(I found I had to wear heels, nylons, and dresses)—but the resistance to women in the workforce had also changed from fear to war. At one company, my male colleagues placed on my desk a picture of a pregnant woman cooking and cleaning; they told me that I should be "barefoot and pregnant in the kitchen." I was mortified but suppressed my emotions; I knew that upsetting me was their intent, and I wouldn't give them the satisfaction. I stayed calm. Recalling my early work experiences, I can now see the essential value of authenticity, and how critical it was that I maintained clear, and strong boundaries. By remaining aware of the environment, accepting my situation, acquiring expertise, adapting to new circumstances, and maintaining the proper attitude, I persevered to succeed as a female pioneer in corporate America. I am now ready to pursue my own adventures.

As women rise to lead governments, major corporations, and large nonprofit organizations, they are subject to significantly more scrutiny than their male counterparts are. This may at first have been seen as either justified or a novelty, but no longer. The media is enthralled with what women leaders are wearing, how they look, and what they are saying. Society values female superficial appearances. Women are supposed to do it all, not only mothers and wives, but also lovers and maintain their appearances. If, for any reason, a woman is deemed to have come up short in any of these multiple endeavors, she is branded forever as being incapably weak. Men, on the other hand, are revered for their heroic endeavors and flaws which are interpreted as building character; whereas female leaders are criticized.

Thousands of years have concretely wired women with an innate ability to juggle several tasks at once. Women are stereotypically considered more emotional—or worse, more *"hormonal"*—than men; however, they tend to think things out before acting. Imagine, for a moment, a world in which we never considered if an individual were male or female. Our expectations of a good result, then, would in no way involve gender. If we work together to remove cultural restrictions on women, their happiness and effectiveness will expand and their natural leadership will be accepted. Actually the happiness of both men and women would increase.

Interview Questions

We interviewed female and male leaders who have developed leadership skills depicting their philosophies, personalities, and visions for success. The participants are:

- Diana Vagelos (Entrepreneur, philanthropist, lecturer, board member)
- Dr. Karl Stevens (Dean of engineering, professor, and author)
- Dr. Brian R. Clement (HHI co-founder, director, lecturer, and author)
- Dr. Susanne Lapp (Chair of university department, professor, and author)
- Lavinia Mears, Esq. (Lawyer, consultant, author, board member)
- Helen (Heidi) D. Reavis, Esq. (Lawyer, film consultant, lecturer, board member).

The seven questions below gave structure to the interviews; however, we allowed them freedom to discuss their philosophy and what they felt was important. Their interviews are interspersed within the sections of the book.

The following are the seven questions we asked:

1. What is the major axiom you follow as a leader that you feel is the most important mantra you use to keep your leadership unique and the secret to your success?

2. What were the major accomplishments that you felt you were happy to have been involved in and how did you achieve these successes?

3. How would you describe your relationship with your closest colleagues and people that you depended on to get the job done?

4. How did you deal with stress and how did you handle conflicts with your team members?

5. How would you describe your career, stages, and what were the major turning points that got you to your highest level?

6. What inspired you and how did you inspire the people who worked with you? How did people help you accomplish your goals?

7. Please feel free to discuss what you feel you would like to communicate about your leadership style, experience or where you are now?

Introduction

Leadership

Authenticity

Boundaries

"*Male and female represent the two sides of the
great radical dualism. But, in fact, they are perpetually
passing into one another. Fluid hardens to solid, solid
rushes to fluid. There is no wholly masculine
man, no purely feminine woman.*"

"*Nature provides exceptions to every rule.
She sends women to battle, and sets Hercules spinning;
she enables women to bear immense burdens, cold, and frost;
she enables the man, who feels maternal love,
to nourish his infant like a mother.*"

"*Our capacities, our instincts for this our present sphere,
are but half developed. Let us be completely natural;
before we trouble ourselves with the supernatural.*"

—MARGARET FULLER, AMERICAN WRITER,
JOURNALIST, AND PHILOSOPHER

Female Leadership Formula

One of the primary goals of this book is to help women understand some of the required attributes for great leadership and to help them develop a healthy balance for work, self, and family. Because women tend to give all they can for others, they have to strike a balance to avoid suffering health consequences.

Our formula is simple: *Authenticity + boundaries = leadership.* With leadership—the true-self—as our goal, we need support systems to keep any leadership structure strong enough to stand the test of time. Authenticity represents the raw building blocks of leadership; boundaries serve as supportive guidelines.

Men tend to support each other in teams, while career women, by necessity, have had to do things alone. As a result, women need mentors and role models to learn more about this process. Our country has evolved from slavery giving every man, black or white, freedom and equal rights through support. Women still have to fight for equal rights and do not support each other as readily. Back in the 1800s, as women began fighting in earnest for equal rights, Margaret Fuller, an early female American journalist, critic, and author, made waves with her courageous book *Women in the Nineteenth Century*. She developed educational discussions with women who had no access to higher education. She is our role model for how women can help other women achieve their personal bests. This book will provide every woman a solid basis and foundation for managing her strong sense of self, to remind her that she has to come first if she hopes to help others later.

We include the following pictorial visions for this book:

1) **For Section One**, imagine an ancient temple (*female leadership*) supported by the attributes of *authenticity* and *boundaries*. Women have the *power* to keep this temple together for eons; they merely have to believe they can. Women tend to be better at practicing authenticity, while males are naturally better with boundaries. Women want the truth—they dislike lies—and have often been the whistleblowers in this country, while men seem better at separating things.

2) **For Section Two**, imagine a *scale* with female attributes on the left side and male attributes on the right side. The Chinese depict this duality as "Yin and Yang", a circle with black and white sides and an opposite color dot in the middle of each side. Ideally we each need a balance of our anima/animus attributes (female/male) within us, uniting our different views to attain success. Our goal is to balance ourselves.

3) **For Section Three**, imagine a *bridge* that crosses a great divide with females, balancing their health, on one side and males, on the other. The female archetype JUSTICE holds a sword in one hand and scales in the other. We need to use our differences to bridge the gap, forging partnerships to become leaders. The suspension bridge may sway but will hold us.

To communicate a vision of the criteria involved in great leadership, we review below the basic concepts of *authenticity* and *boundaries.*

Authenticity is critical to reaching your individual best. Without authenticity, our creative-self cannot blossom; without awareness, truth, and understanding, the true-self cannot survive. Along with authenticity, boundaries play key roles in setting limits for relationships, participation, and connection. Boundaries limit the chaos and confusion that great leaders must navigate around. Confusion begets paralysis that stymies the completion of tasks and the fulfillment of goals. Authenticity and boundaries are the mainstays for great leadership.

It's true that the whole is greater than the sum of the parts; only if we work together to become a "whole" can we become truly, authentically powerful. Authenticity and boundaries are important parts that preclude manipulative and superficial behavior. Great leadership is the result.

Authenticity

---

*"Presenting leadership as a list of carefully defined
qualities (like strategic, analytical, and performance-oriented)
no longer holds; instead, true leadership stems
from individuality that is honestly and sometimes
imperfectly expressed. Leaders should strive
for authenticity over perfection."*

*"Leadership is not bullying and leadership is
not aggression. Leadership is the expectation that you
can use your voice for good; that you can
make the world a better place."*

*"I think now is our time.
My mother was told by everyone that
she had two choices: She could be a nurse or a teacher.
The external barriers now are just so much lower.
If we start acknowledging what the real issues are,
we can solve them. It's not that hard."*

—SHERYL SANDBERG,
CHIEF OPERATING OFFICER OF
FACEBOOK, AUTHOR OF "LEAN IN"

Becoming a great leader requires, first, becoming truly authentic
and responsible—without superficial tendencies. Superficiality per-
tains to the surface—what's shallow or untrue; authenticity, on the
other hand, refers to a person's fundamental depth. Authenticity is

the real thing—in Latin, *bona fide* or "good faith"—and involves being genuine, truthful, real, and trustworthy. People recognize statements that are exaggerated, untrue, or unrealistic. Lord Byron, a British poet, said: *"Truth is a gem that is found at a great depth; whilst on the surface of this world all things are weighed by the false scale of custom."* As opposed to *falsity, authenticity* also implies something that lasts forever—as constant and strong as the Parthenon in Greece, the Celtic dolmens, or the pyramids in Egypt. That kind of authenticity lends structure and support to your own consistent and realistic behavior, enabling you to focus on the task at hand.

We propose seven major axioms regarding authenticity:

- **False premises fade away.** Being authentic implies that despite external pressures, stress, or problems, you remain true to your own personality, spirit, or character and have a strong sense of self. Eleanor Roosevelt, for example, represented the plight of the disenfranchised with a spirit of authenticity. She was indomitable in her pursuit of justice. The image of Winston Churchill, another great leader, lasts through the decades due to his genuineness and trust-worthiness. Churchill won the trust of the world as a global leader who persevered through tough times. His personality, responsibilities, and boundaries were clear when dealing with other great global leaders. We reference his strength (he told it like it was, without lies) and authentic character to this day.

- **Superficiality precludes authenticity.** Continually changing one's mind at a whim without presenting a consistent and strong character often reveals a weakness for superficiality. Strength and depth are reflected in consistency of vision. Unfortunately, western culture generally rewards superficiality, since we sometimes have difficulty discerning fact from fiction. There are clear exceptions, of course, such as Pope Francis. The first Vatican leader to hail from Argentina, Pope Francis displays an honest and humble demeanor that continues to surprise the world as he opposes the greed and selfish behavior apparent in many corporate and political leaders. Truth and connection are signs of his honest authenticity. Following examples such as his, we can practice becoming authentic until it becomes a natural state of mind.

- **Authenticity is derived from strong character.** A strong character implies a confident, noble, motivated, brave, and courageous leader—one who is willing to take risks while remaining truthful. For example, Christine Lagarde, managing director of the International Monetary Fund, continues to explain in simple terms how to solve our economic crisis. Leaders of her caliber solve complex problems by breaking them down into simple concepts, a process that demands courage and requires the abilities to identify truth, recognize honesty, and dismiss anything superficial. Superficiality implies being easily influenced by external events, lacking the internal strength (or depth) to stay the course. Strength of character resides within the personal self; its development involves high self-esteem, trust, and belief in self.

- **Authentic people are truthful.** Authenticity is the opposite of confusion. Truthfully embracing your feelings, beliefs, and attitudes will help support your authentic self—a separate, unique, consistent, and trustworthy person. When heads of state promise to deliver changes and nothing happens, we learn not to trust them. Lies obviously represent a flawed method of communication; the truth inevitably emerges, and anyone who becomes known as "a liar" is hobbled in leading others. Lies erode the glue of truthful spiritual energy; even though one might feel a measure of control while lying, that control is fleeting. It will dissipate when the truth comes out. And remember the old folktale of "crying wolf" too many times: Even if a true threat emerges, people known to be liars are rarely heeded, and are often even shunned.

- **Great leaders inspire others.** Leaders motivate others to see the truth for themselves. A leader's beliefs and vision support a strong sense of self that is integrated and authentic; a leader has strong boundaries, and is able to act nobly in the face of fear or uncertainty. India's Mahatma Gandhi, for example, never allowed his vision or belief to waver; he exhibited remarkable patience as the world witnessed his stamina to gain independence for his country. Who he was, and what he believed, was clear to all. His love of peace overcame all. He remained consistent until his silent behavior broke down every barrier. To this day, his actions connote great strength, wisdom, patience, vision, and a persistent attitude in service of his beliefs.

- **Great leaders also take the initiative.** Leaders are aware of those around them, and realize that actions have consequences. They take initiatives to ensure that their followers are on board. They are confident that they have the vision to see a problem clearly, and to generate solutions. Great leaders have clear intentions, inspiration, and vision. For example, both male and female leaders can be our role models, but women have traditionally had limited access to leadership positions. We are grateful that the modern era is finally beginning to acknowledge women's accomplishments, but women leaders must take the initiative, and must press even harder to make inroads.

- **Authenticity implies awareness of self and environment.** Authentic leaders have to be aware of their surroundings so that they can remain truthful and pursue their goals unaffected by what other people do. Professional golf champion Rory McIlroy, for example, has stated that it is important for him to keep focused on what he is doing and not worry about what others are doing. Also Maria Sharapova, a tennis champion takes a few seconds for herself (turning her back to the other player) between points to establish her sense of self.

The following 5 As represent qualities needed by leaders:

1) **Awareness**—Cognition and observation allow you to take note of your actions and behavior, and to react to any effects they may have on others or on your own circumstances. Awareness breeds intelligence.

2) **Acceptance**—Readiness to accept changes and to adapt to

unexpected situations enables you to remain in control to make contingencies. Without accepting what is, you cannot move forward to the next level.

3) **Acquirement**—Readiness to learn new things, and to listen to others to acquire new knowledge, no matter how upsetting, will help you authentically adjust and readjust to circumstances. Being prepared helps you to take required next steps.

4) **Adaptation**—Knowledge that things are always moving will help you accept any changes and enable you to incorporate new protocols and regulations without blame or complaints. Living in the past prevents moving toward the future.

5) **Attitude**—Knowledge that you can't control what happens, but can control your responses to things, events, and people will help you stay positive and maintain readiness. Growing increases the ability to connect to others.

When deploying these 5 As, authentic leaders behave both nobly and responsibly—espousing real truths that are timeless. People intuitively understand when leaders are superficial or not compassionate. Any leader must have a strong and established persona that promotes truth in order to inspire others and address their needs. Great leaders in sports, for example, such as tennis champions Rafael Nadal , and Chris Evert, as well as golf champion Phil Mickelson, are truthful and noble in their actions, in and out of the sports arenas. Their dedication and devotion to helping youth around the world, as well as their work ethic, are unsurpassed, making them great leaders and inspiring role models.

Boundaries

"Leadership is a series of behaviors rather than a role for heroes. When leaders take back power, when they act as heroes and saviors, they end up exhausted, overwhelmed, and deeply stressed."

"Even though worker capacity and motivation are destroyed when leaders choose power over productivity, it appears that bosses would rather be in control than have the organization work well."

"Listening is such a simple act. It requires us to be present, and that takes practice, but we don't have to do anything else. We don't advise, or coach, or sound wise. Listening is a reciprocal process—we become more attentive to others if they have attended to us."

—MARGARET J. WHEATLEY, AUTHOR, ORGANIZATIONAL AND MANAGEMENT CONSULTANT

Many female writers have produced books on leadership, but Margaret Wheatley's 2002 book *Turning to One Another* really hits home. A major requirement for great leadership is an authentic acceptance of clear boundaries for each participant to bring to the table. Clear boundaries help us become authentic leaders; knowing our limits enables us to behave accordingly. Wheatley, an organizational behaviorist, won an award in 2003 for: "Distinguished

Contribution to Workplace Learning and Performance." She has received many awards, honorary degrees, and has traveled around the globe as an advisor for leadership initiatives.

Boundary-guided behaviors support *congruency* or the ability to grow together without overpowering others. Virginia Satir, a well-known family psychotherapist, gauged congruency by measuring awareness, acknowledgement, and acceptance of feelings. Congruency relies on boundaries. Suzanne Welstead, a family therapist, wrote the book, *Searching for You* (2009). She explains: "*Our bodies, thoughts, and feelings are aligned together which creates a whole (not partial) response to a given situation. We are an integrated people living from a solid inner foundation that is complete*". She continues: "*Congruency is a sound and satisfying place from which to relate to others, and creates trust and stability in relationships.*" Integrated people have the best chance to become authentic when they are responsible for—and congruent with—their own boundaries. Boundaries support congruency.

We propose seven major axioms regarding boundaries:

- **Boundaries are critical.** Many theorists expound on the importance of boundaries, including those of the self, and of those between men and women. Men and women can work together with respect for their differences and for different approaches to the task at hand; these differences don't require changing the other person or insisting on only one way to do things. Boundaries are similar to rules, procedures, and regulations regarding the act of working together and communication. There can be confusion when multiple people express opinions; boundaries can simplify, and are required for

development of excellent communication skills to complete
tasks and achieve success for leaders and followers.

- **Your boundaries are as unique as you are.** Being a great
  leader requires inspiring others to be who they are—or, more
  important, who they can best be—without fear of closing
  themselves off or violating their boundaries. Your boundaries are your own—you cannot change the innate behavior
  of another person, only your own behaviors. Your job is to
  be clear about your limitations, needs, and boundaries for
  success. Great leaders know who they are and what they
  can expect from others. They have a clear vision. Any self-
  confusion or lack of self-control—the inability to assume
  responsibility for one's actions—is a sign of problems
  comprehending boundaries. No one is perfect, but realizing
  one's limitations helps clarify problem-solving.

- **Clear boundaries inspire trust.** When we lack boundaries,
  our power is diminished; we no longer have the ability to
  inspire, and our leadership potential is damaged. In their
  book, *Boundaries: When to Say Yes, How to Say No to Take
  Control of Your Life*, Henry Cloud and John Townsend
  stated: "*our spiritual and emotional well-being depends
  on our ability to cultivate the spirit of forming responsible
  boundaries.*" Responsible boundaries inspire trust and
  authentic relationships. Great leaders need strong and clear
  boundaries; their own problems and issues must not confuse
  others or cause complexity in solving problems. Any personal
  complexity imposed upon problem-solving issues leads to
  failure and mistrust. Clarity of vision inspires trust.

- **Clear boundaries also limit chaos.** Great leaders heed boundaries and set limits to avoid creating chaos. Chaos occurs when insecurities and lack of confidence or self-esteem loom among individuals. Everyone in a team has to put aside self-centered and security (control) issues. Boundary issues often reveal problems with responsibility. Being responsible in your work and with your family helps you build strong boundaries. A leader must be—and behave as—a separate being in order to respond properly and productively to another being or entity. Great leaders have clear visions, well-defined limits, and a devotion to noble acts that inspire others to be courageous and do heroic deeds. Boundaries help in defining parameters for behavior.

- **Different types of boundaries exist.** Personal boundaries define the parts of ourselves that we protect from the chaos of the outside world. Having people near you that support this process is paramount. If you surround yourself with people who criticize you, judge you, or put you down, you will find yourself powerless and feeling subordinate. Weak people who use your energy will weaken you. We also need to be truthful; this can help us maintain boundaries that are clear and strong. We move quickly in this world of global connections, and sometimes we treat this frictionless existence as an escape from conflicts on boundaries. In the face of this, we must remain vigilant: We must be responsible with our actions, reminding ourselves that behaviors have consequences and can hurt others.

- **Different types of leaders are visible in every realm.** There are great leaders in every discipline—politics, sports, business, fashion, art, and elsewhere. The different boundaries discussed above are relevant in any field, and critical to advancing the role as a leader in any realm. It is the responsibility of each leader to make these boundaries clear and to make sure everyone on the team knows what needs to be done. Each type of leadership still has to connect with each person in the team. The leader is only one part of the team. Each member of the team is integral for job completion. Clarity breeds success.

- **Clear boundaries rely on good intentions.** Intention helps you connect easily without conflict and with free-flowing energy. Personal boundaries provide behavioral guidelines that define limits in the physical, mental, and emotional parts of self—boundaries that are often different in men and women. Great leaders are able to exist in their respective genderless spiritual domains, and interact with others, without losing themselves. Each of the following three aspects of the integrated self is fraught with unique issues and concerns when relating to other people:

Aspect of Self	Defined By	Boundaries Involve
Physical	your persona, the outside self which others first see, and its interaction with others	teams, interpersonal structure
Emotional	your emotions (true feelings), and the separation from manipulative actions of others	trust, loyalty, delegating power
Mental	your own thoughts and opinions irrespective of others' approval	confidence, efficacy, mastering self

Taken together, these three aspects reveal the spiritual self. The boundaries of the spiritual self are implicitly understood; they allow both genders to meet without conflict. Within our own boundaries, we cannot be subject to self-sabotage; we can manage our weaknesses and trust others. For example, when asked to name the most important axiom in his leadership role, the ex-CEO of a Fortune 500 company replied, "to trust my people." Great leaders depend on great followers. Boundary issues can compromise goals and target dates, as well as integrity.

Authenticity and boundaries in balance are necessary factors for women to become great leaders. (Women can learn the boundaries part from men, who tend to have that part down pat; men, in turn, can learn from our natural authenticity virtues.) Authenticity and boundaries are the pillars that guide us through the vicissitudes of work, life, and family. We are the models for our children and everyone we come into contact with in our daily lives. We can only be the best we can be if we give ourselves strong foundations that sustain our confidence, courage, and commitment to accomplish our goals. Men have their "old boys' club" to support each other; women, on the other hand, have for centuries had a tendency to compete with each other, fiercely protecting their respective domains. But we are all global now; we are in each other's backyards; we are interdependent. We must now evolve to support each other if we want our communities and our world to survive. Our boundaries must evolve as well, to reflect the new paradigm.

Health is the number-one priority for all; without it we cannot be happy or fully realized. Women must feel passion for their work; without it we will experience stress and an unhealthy lifestyle. That passion, when misapplied toward feeling needed or connected, generally leads women to give of themselves beyond what is necessary. We have to educate women to give some regard to self, and to develop the self-respect required to balance their workloads. Women also have to develop authentic selves, with clear boundaries, to keep sexual discrimination from entering their work environment.

The dire predicament facing American culture can only be remedied if we work together to change bias, prejudice, and negative opinions through education. Men and women can learn from each other to keep their male/female balance in check. In particular, however, women need to support other women. They must free themselves from the narrow view that women are limited solely to domestic or subservient roles. All women must strike a balance for themselves, whether that means dedicating part of their lives to children or another part to a career or to the great responsibility of leadership—or overlapping some or all of those efforts in a meaningful way. Running a household, after all, also requires leadership skills.

Section One

....

Women and Leadership

"In the long run, we shape our lives,
and we shape ourselves. The process never ends
until we die. And the choices we make are
ultimately our own responsibility."

"You gain strength, courage, and confidence
by every experience in which you really stop to look
fear in the face. You are able to say to yourself,
'I lived through this horror. I can take the
next thing that comes along.' "

"No one can make you feel inferior
without your consent."

—ELEAANOR ROOSEVELT
AMERICAN POLITIAN, FIRST LADY
AND LEADER OF HUMAN RIGHTS

Female Leaders in History

Throughout history, women have been balancing work and home life. This is a mark of true leadership, an individual formula for each woman. Women in our culture have to fit their individual family and work lives into societal expectations; some, however, have managed to achieve success as great leaders—leaders that we believe are under-represented in our curricula. America, in fact, has lagged behind the rest of the world, in which women have long been able to achieve top-level positions of power. Europe has been doing it for over a thousand years and Africa for even longer. In South America right now, women preside over several countries. The month of March has been dedicated as Women's History Month, which we hope will focus much-needed attention on the contributions females have made to the world. This is our chance to enumerate many heroines. It is time to claim our rights and become powerful leaders in the world. American society is ready for these changes. We are ready for a female president to join the ranks of global leaders.

Women have seen themselves as powerless for generations; since World War II, however, they have realized that they are strong, committed, and able to do the work of men. During the war years, our country counted on women to do the difficult jobs which had been held by the men before heading overseas—and the women did very well; we won the war with women doing most of the jobs required. In the 1960s, women entering the workforce had to adapt to male standards of behavior and dress. Their feminine ways were rejected in that context; they found they were only able to achieve recognition and trust from their male counterparts by becoming better than those men were at the same jobs.

Women are clearly capable of competing in the new corporate games to become great leaders, but only a handful of them have risen to the very highest levels. Some recent leaders, such as Facebook's Sheryl Sandberg (with her book *Lean In*) and General Motors' Mary Barra (the automotive industry's first female CEO), are making great strides, but only three percent of Fortune 500 companies are now led by women CEOs—hardly a huge increase from the one percent figure reported in the 1990s.

PART I

. . . .

HISTORY OF FEMALE LEADERSHIP

"IT IS NOT EASY TO BE A PIONEER—BUT OH, IT IS FASCINATING!
I WOULD NOT TRADE ONE MOMENT, EVEN THE WORST
MOMENT, FOR ALL THE RICHES IN THE WORLD."

—Elizabeth Blackwell
(the first woman in the United States to earn a medical degree)

Our history of female leadership starts with ancient times and the middle ages, and continues through the Renaissance, the Enlightenment, and into the modern era.

We know that women were revered, had status, and were held in high esteem thousands of years ago. In ancient times, there were many female physicians, scientists, and astronomers, such as:

- Merit-Ptah (2700 BC), a physician in ancient Egypt and perhaps the first woman known by name in the history of medicine;

- Agamede (12th century BC), the first female physician to practice legally in Athens; and
- Aglaonike (2nd century BC), the first female astronomer in ancient Greece. She predicted lunar eclipses.

As far back as the 8th century BC, Homer noted the great accomplishments of female warriors, such as Dido the queen of Carthage (840 BC–760 BC), and the Amazons. There were many stories of heroic exploits such as, the Trojan War to recapture Helen of Troy. It is reported that women had a lot more freedom than women of today.

Women in Ancient History

Around 500 BC, women in ancient Greece (before the Hellenic period) had great status, owned land, and were politically involved with more power than they did at the end of the BC era. Hypatia, a Greek philosopher and scientist living in Alexandria (fourth century AD) was thought to be a witch and was killed for her beliefs, political power, and teachings. We know about the history that has been written about female witches, as evil and against God, even though they were just strong women, powerful, and doing male work. Women had much more freedom in Etruria, northern Italy (the Etruscans), as well as the Celtics. The era around 500 BC depicted powerful women. For example, there were several female scientists such as, Artemsia, a Greek botanist, from Caria in 300 BC, and other female physicians.

Sapho (620–570 BC), a poet and philosopher, taught young women in her academy as Lesvos music, singing, poetry, and social behavior.

The Etruscan Women

In the centuries before the rise of Rome, the Etruscan culture flourished, producing great educators, architects, and scientists. (Rome's early buildings and aqueducts, in fact, are attributed to the skills of the Etruscans.) The Etruscan era lasted from roughly the 8th century BC until Rome became more powerful around 300 BC. Though the Etruscans' power diminished during the rise of northern Italy's many city-states, they were considered the most advanced society with higher education and engineering skills. They had an incredible navy and ruled almost all of Italy as a superpower.

Etruscan wives were treated with respect and dignity during religious outings and in public, attending symposiums alone or with their husbands. They loved to weave and had many home-based industries; however, they loved their freedom and were allowed to ride horses and own chariots—scandalous acts in the rest of the world at that time. These women were not subject to being "owned"; they passed their names onto their children and controlled their own bodies. They felt each person was a gift to each other and respected human rights.

Etruscan women were "free" in a manner not seen again until relatively recently; they enjoyed a measure of independence and equality that remains unmatched to this day. Even though most writers and philosophers of the time considered them scandalous and vain—they were, for example, supposedly too enamored of their etched bronze mirrors—they were powerful, respected, and had legal rights. But the mirrors helped the Etruscan women achieve a separate sense of self, with etchings of myths and of people sharing their thoughts with letters floating through the air. Their communication and boundaries of self all seem far more advanced than our modern psychological sense of self. In fact, we have a lot to learn from the Etruscans. The women were key members of a happy, brilliant society. They loved learning, were more literate than even their Greek counterparts, and had high social and political status. Their sarcophagi depicted joyful, realistic statues of couples on top sharing their lounge thrones equally, and participating in banquets as expressed around the bottom. We are trying in our societal culture to be happily married without divorce—something the Etruscans mastered.

Powerful Role Models

The Etruscan women (900–200 BC) had status and held high level political positions. They were independent and the role models for ancient Greek or Roman women who were also powerful, owned land, and held offices. During these ancient times, trading was the more important pastime and not empire building. Wars were only defensive, while learning, sharing, and trading were valued. Aspasia from the first century was also a Greek physician becoming a role model for many Greek female scientists such as, Hypatia (4th century astronomer, philosopher, and mathematician) living in the Greek city of Alexandria, Egypt.

Celtic women were warriors around the early AD years, such as Queen Boudica who died fighting the Romans around 60 AD. There were many queens in history as mothers of future kings such as, in Egypt, and other nations in Africa where they were called *Queen Mothers* or regents ruling when children were too young to rule. Other queens, like Cleopatra, managed to cut out their competitions for the throne, including siblings. She managed to become a key player as part of the Roman Empire. Many Greek women in ancient times were scientists and physicians. They were taught by the greatest scientists, mathematicians, and philosophers.

African Female Leaders

Hatshepsut (fifteenth century BC) was the first female queen of Egypt and very powerful as she assumed the title of Pharaoh reserved for men only. She promoted the arts and trade and built a beautiful temple Deir el-Bahri near Thebes. Amina was a Nigerian queen in the sixteenth century and was a great military leader and opened trade routes to the south enriching Zaria's economy with gold, slaves and cola nuts. Sammuramat was an Assyrian queen in the ninth century BC who was both wife and mother of kings known for accompanying her husband into battles expanding Babylonia's control over many territories near the Tigris and Euphrates rivers, as well as, restoring the beauty of her capital. Women were powerful during this era.

There was also an African queen (Bathsheba) who married King David during the early biblical era. During the early Christian era, the mother of Emperor Constantine the Great ruled in the fourth century AD and later he ruled with his mother St. Helena by his side. Once Christianity began with the birth of Christ, we have two dominant women in the New Testament: The Virgin Mary (the mother of Christ) and Mary Magdalene (*the prostitute who was forgiven*). They gave birth to what some psychologists refer to as the *Madonna/Whore complex* where men can't have sex as readily with their wives (who are mothers) and prefer other women since they regard them symbolically as "*whores.*" We acknowledge that we have come a long way and this bias towards women has faded a bit yet the stigma holds as men who cheat say, "*it meant nothing.*" This connects to the complex (mothers/wives are viewed as holy or not prone to their sexual gratification). We understand the dilemma, but maybe they can adjust to new feelings.

Female Educators and Pioneers

Some women were educated as far back as ancient times and during the middle ages many were allowed to study in abbeys. Women were also warriors and educators during the early Christian times; some women participated in the Crusades. The first university was founded in Bologna in 1088 AD; we know women attended the school throughout the middle ages. In 1678, Elena Cornaro Piscopia (1646–1684) became one of the first women to receive a doctoral degree from a university, studying theology and earning a doctorate in Philosophy from the University of Padua. During the enlightenment era of the eighteenth century, many educated women wrote significant treatises and essays, as well as novels. Émilie du Châtelet of France (1706–1749) was a great author, scientist, mathematician, and philosopher who is renowned today for her advanced work. She was also a colleague of Voltaire, with whom she collaborated on treatises. She was encouraged by Voltaire to continue her work with and without him.

Early Christian Leaders

Christians have come to understand their great heritage and their foibles. We know the Catholic Church is dealing with the ramifications of the abuse of children from priests who use their power to seduce the innocent. Power is not a game. It is a responsibility. Around the sixth century AD, Christianity flourished and the reign of Justinian The First began with his well-known wife, Theodora, (a beautiful woman) and empress of the Roman (Byzantine) Empire. They rebuilt the city (known before as Byzantium) called Constantinople (known now as Istanbul). She was one of the most powerful and influential rulers of the Byzantine Empire. Besides her religious beliefs (Greek Orthodoxy), and connection to the people, she created her own centers of power (Hagia or Saint Sophia Church). Her interesting story and her rise to power is similar to Eva Peron of Argentina. Women around the globe for centuries have made their mark on history.

During the eleventh century, the orthodox religion split from the catholic religion due to certain discrepancies. The major reasons included that the Christian orthodox religion did not recognize the pope as its supreme ruler and rejected the statues that were part of the catholic churches and cathedrals. They also disagreed with celibacy for the priests. Orthodox priests are allowed to marry. Catholics thought that celibacy was needed to have a higher connection with God; however, how can we explain the abuse of children by catholic priests. This is the highest example of abuse of power which is projected onto innocent victims by using the name of God. This is real heresy and if they burned witches for less, what should they do to these priests? The answer is unresolved and these culprits are often protected.

Powerful Women of the Middle Ages

There were many powerful women in the aristocracy of the middle ages who achieved power. Women in this period were generally used as pawns by their wealthy families or royal as child-bearers to arranged dynastic marriages. There was Olga (Helga) of Russia the first known woman to rule Russia and she adopted Christianity (the Orthodox Church). She was the widow of Igor The First and became regent queen with her son. There were many female saints such as, Saint Matilda, founder of monasteries and builder of churches who became the Queen of Germany as the wife of Henry I. Also, there is Saint Edith of Polesworth, daughter of Edward of England and the widow of the King of Dublin and York who became a nun at Polesworth Abbey.

One of the most famous queens of this period was Eleanor of Aquitaine (1122–1204 AD) who had two different husbands (King Louis of France and Henry II of England). She ruled France from 1137 to 1152 AD (accompanying her husband on his second crusade) and she ruled England from 1154 to 1189 AD. She was powerful and gave birth to the future King of England, Richard I the Lionhearted. She was queen consort during each of her marriages and became regent when her son became king. She is considered one of the most powerful women in the middle ages.

During the middle ages, the Vikings attacked many lands including England and Ireland. Ethelfleda (869–918 AD) was the daughter of King Alfred the Great (849–899 AD) who was a warrior and politically powerful. Northern Europeans were in battle trying to protect their lands; however, during this time there were many women politicians, warriors and pirates. Tamar (1160–1214 AD) was the queen regent of Georgia (near Russia) and although a woman. she was regarded as King Tamar by the people of Mercia. She achieved great military conquests such as, parts of Turkey, Persia, as well as parts of Russia and Armenia. Also, in the tenth century, there was Thyra of Denmark who was the consort queen of King Gorm and led an army against the Germans. Many female warriors who were Scandinavian had fought to protect their lands. Also, at this time there were many Persian female military warriors and tacticians. They were brave, bright, talented, and skillful strategists, who fought just as hard, if not more so, than their male counterparts.

Women Leaders of the Renaissance Era

Some women during the Renaissance period were heroines such as, Joan of Arc winning freedom for France in the fifteenth century. Also Isabella d'Este (1474–1539) was known as the "First Lady of the Renaissance". She was well educated, speaking many languages, and after her husband died, she ruled the city state of Mantua (Italy), showing great leadership and political skills. She encouraged the arts and women to break away from traditional roles. Another great lady of the renaissance, Catherine de Medici was born in Florence in 1519 and married the King of France in 1533 and she became Queen Regent. She helped built a new wing of the Louvre museum and was instrumental as patron of the arts. There was Queen Elizabeth I (1558–1603) of England who was feared and considered a formidable female leader rivaling male leaders of the time. She did not marry and she maintained her independence. She is considered the great monarch in English history since she preserved peace and stability at a personal cost. Her pride stood strong and she remained dominate for almost fifty years.

There are many global female leaders throughout the ages. Most contributed to humanity and continued to as we end the renaissance and enter the period of enlightenment. We can keep enumerating them but we will only mention the few that we see as good examples. America needs to catch up and hopefully this can be accomplished in our lifetime. Mary Queen of Scots (1542–1587) claimed that she was the rightful heir to the throne of England and she suffered with an unstable and insecure life. As a child she was sent to France to marry King Francis II who died and she was forced to flee due to religious wars as she was a catholic and ultimately executed by Queen Elizabeth (1558–1603) after 19 years of being imprisoned. She was caught in the middle of wars between Scotland and England; however, her son King James I became king of England. Much has been written about Queen Mary of Scotland and Queen Elizabeth The First.

Queen Elizabeth I succeeded her half-sister in 1558 and depended on a group of trusted advisors. She started the Church of England and since she didn't marry she became known as "The Virgin Queen." She was associated with many affairs which seemed to help her and she won the war with Spain considered the greatest military victory in English history. Her ruling motto was *video et taceo* (I see and say nothing); however, she had plenty of help getting help accomplishing her goals. She was alleged to be in love with her childhood friend Robert Dudley but she never married to secure her power. She was charismatic, short-tempered and cautious in foreign affairs. She manipulated suitors to gain and preserve her power.

Leaders of the Enlightenment Era

The enlightenment period was led by France in Europe with great philosophers of that era. One of its dominant ladies was Emilie du Chatelet who was born in 1706. We continue to note her work as a brilliant French mathematician, physicist, translator, and author during the Age of Enlightenment (eighteenth century). She translated Isaac Newton's work *Principia Mathematica*. She learned and debated with Voltaire (well-known French philosopher and author) who said her only fault was that she was a woman. Emilie continued with many scientific revelations and published numerous findings from her research. For example, she wrote a paper on the nature of fire that predicted what is known today as infrared radiation and the nature of light. We barely hear about her accomplishments. She was ahead of her time and her scientific papers apply today. There is not enough paper to enumerate her work.

Mary Wollstonecraft (1759–1797), an English wife, mother, philosopher, author, and the first female feminist, was a well-respected outspoken advocate and laid the groundwork for others to follow. She is credited with saying that *"virtue can only flourish among equals,"* and that *"It is justice, not charity, that is wanting in the world."* She wrote a book *A Vindication of the Rights of Woman* which advocated for social reforms and for women's equality: "*I do not wish women to have power over men; but over themselves.* . . . *Independence I have long considered as the grand blessing of life, the basis of every virtue; and independence I will ever secure by contracting my wants, though I were to live on a barren heath.*"

During the eighteenth century, Europe was experiencing the enlightenment period where everyone wanted to learn about the arts and the advanced culture of philosophy and knowledge. One of the female leaders of this period was Catherine the Great of Russia (1729–1796) who ruled from 1762 till her death, the longest female monarch in Russia. She was known for being a great empress, expanding the borders of her country, and for bringing in the great thinkers of the time to her court. She transformed herself into a great empress through sheer determination and continued the Westernization of Russia started by Peter the Great. Catherine had ambition, courage with great intelligence and was political in building alliances through hard work. She became a great leader working for the welfare of all and saved her people by using small pox vaccination to help millions. Catherine the Great was also known for her social reform. She built a powerful support team that helped her rule successfully.

Women's rights were somehow relaxed during the Renaissance and Enlightenment eras; during the first half of the nineteenth century, women started fighting openly for their rights. The suffrage movement (mid-1800s–1920s), for example, saw women pushing for the right to vote. Margaret Fuller (1810–1850) was considered the first American suffrage activist and the first female journalist sent to Europe. She was also an editor and critic—the first full-time American female book reviewer, in fact—and author of *Woman in the Nineteenth Century*. An advocate of women's rights to education and to employment, she started groups to help educate those who were deprived of higher education. She was also the role model for Susan B. Anthony (1820–1906), an American social reformer who led the women's suffrage movement and whose followers set the nation on fire until women were granted the right to vote in 1920.

Women and WWII

The history of powerful women in the modern era starts after WWII (worked jobs of men during war) and we review women leaders into the twenty-first century. One great male leader Winston Churchill stated: *"To every man there comes in his lifetime that special moment when he is figuratively tapped on the shoulder and offered that chance to do a very special thing, unique to him and fitted to his talents."* We would like to add not only to every man but to every woman and change the "he" to "she" or "him"/"his" to "her". Women had to do the jobs of men who were absent because of the war. They became powerful once the new feelings of independence and capability became theirs. We can only review the female leaders that are documented. As time goes by, we are discovering more great female leaders from the past; however, like seekers of truth in an archeological dig, we can only find those buried beneath the dust of great male leaders. We know they are there, hidden beneath the debris; however we can also learn from our male leaders. Together we can uncover the truth.

Women and Noble Actions

Noble acts come from authentic people who have a strong sense of self and are not dependent on the weaknesses of others to feel good. Noble acts come from heart and soul of the real self. As an American philosopher Alfred A. Montapert said, *"Your life will be no better than the plans you make and the action you take. You are the architect and builder of your own life, fortune and destiny."* We, as women, always put others first since we are programmed to take care of children whether we have them or not. Noble acts come from strong healthy persons who can judge what is good for others without hurting themselves. For example, Abigail Adams (1744–1818), wife of President John Adams, wrote letters giving advice on government and politics. She supported her husband through the revolutionary war years and helped mend drifts between him and Jefferson. He sought her intellectual and emotional approval; her noble acts included her insistence about not forgetting women and their rights. They collaborated.

Women are now learning they are not victims or subjects for male domination. They can afford to be noble as they climb the social ladder and keep achieving their goals and higher levels of leadership. Noble acts can be spiritual and not concerned with the physical or emotional realm. Women are taught to take care of others and they are the natural caregivers; however, many men are now staying at home and taking care of the children as their wives work. Some share the chores and women are now open to more choices. Men and women are learning to do noble acts with their families and their work as a team. We believe in working together.

Humility and Female Leaders

The ancients seemed to have understood human behavior and how to be the best we can be. Lao Tsu wrote: "*Nobility is rooted in humility, and high founded on low. This is why true lords and emperors call themselves orphaned, destitute, ill-fated. Isn't this rooted in humility? Isn't it?*" Do we understand humility? We seem to be engrossed in having power which can lead to corruption and greed. Our modern notion of nobility has changed to adapt to our selfish acts without concern for the betterment of humanity. There is no real understanding of noble actions or its significance and it is why we ignore noble behavior and do not recognize it. Truly great leaders had some form of nobility in their stature, in their compassion and their ability to adapt to change. They were not afraid to be brave. Noble actions breed great leadership.

Great leaders are noble in their actions when they consider the needs of others in the context of getting the job done. We all have needs; however, noble leaders adapt to changes and fulfill the needs of their followers, even if not economical or achievable. Leaders see that change means flexibility to accept incoming information or problems that can affect outcomes. Great leaders build teams with people they can trust who do not have selfish needs as a priority. For example, Mother Theresa spent her life being generous of herself to accomplish her world of goodness for others. These are noble acts. Another example is Helen Keller, who spent her life devoted to helping others who were also blind or challenged, giving her knowledge to help others in need. She and her companion helped millions find the best of them-selves. Her theme was to never give up and to pursue your dream no matter what it takes. She is a great leader.

Women Leaders of Early Modern Era

During the nineteenth century in England, Queen Victoria ruled most of the century along with her husband Albert who spear-headed many social reforms, especially for the poor and lower middle classes. Queen Victoria is the longest ruling monarch in England and her work with Albert was revolutionary for that time. They developed an empire *"where the sun never sets."* In America, Susan B. Anthony (1820–1906) and Elizabeth Cady Stanton founded America's suffragette movement. After 1900, the movement argued for reforms of the Progressive era. The battle raged in many countries. In New York City, the 1911 disaster of the Triangle Shirtwaist Factory where over 100 women died since they were locked in their work stations and could not escape when fire broke out. People all over the country were outraged.

During the 1960s and 1970s, we had female heroes such as, Emma Peel from the British spy drama *The Advengers* played by Diana Rigg, portraying an intelligent, brave, karate expert. Other examples of feminist role models were *The Mary Tyler Moore Show,* and *That Girl,* played by Marlo Thomas,. Both shows depicted young, independent career women, living on their own in large cities. Wonen are still struggling to maintain their independence. The passage of the Nineteenth Amendment was finally done in 1920 and American women got to vote nationally in the 1922 presidential campaign. The ERA

(Equal Rights Amendment) started in the middle of the twentieth century and is still going on since the bill was never fully ratified.

Female Authors

As for literature, Jane Austen (1775–1817) was a prolific English writer who described women who had few rights or choices. She was a skilled novelist revered by many even today. Her best-known novels, including *Pride and Prejudice* and *Sense and Sensibility*, depict proud men and intelligent women who had moral insight within their limited freedom. She reiterated in all her novels the plight of women with no birth rights or freedom. Another English novelist was Mary Shelley, daughter of the feminist and philosopher Mary Wollstonecraft. Mary Shelley (1797–1851) was known for her gothic novel *Frankenstein*. She was married to the poet Percy Shelley who was friends with Lord Byron. They had spent summers together and encouraged Shelly to write. An English author, Frances Hodgson Burnett (1849–1924), wrote *The Secret Garden* inspiring young children to find the essence of self and identity. Swedish children's author Astrid Lindgren (1907–2002) was an activist for animal and children's rights, and wrote the Pippi Longstocking series of adventures and the popular *Karlsson on the Roof* series.

The Bronte sisters, Charlotte (1816–1855) and Emily (1818–1848), became successful English authors who started writing with male names to become published. Charlotte, the first to succeed, wrote *Jane Eyre*; later, Emily wrote *Wuthering Heights*. Both novels became films that are still being produced and classics in literature. Louisa

May Alcott (1832–1888) was an American author, abolitionist, and feminist who wrote *Little Women*, the first volume of which appeared in 1868. She wrote about love, war, and the plight of working women. Another American author, Edith Wharton (1862–1937 AD) was a close friend of Henry James (an American author) and she wrote *The House of Mirth* and *Ethan Frome* (1911). She was acclaimed for her psychological novels and short stories; however, they emphasized depressed women who were victims of their era and societal expectations. Wharton won a Pulitzer Prize and was nominated for the Nobel Prize in Literature in 1927, 1928, and 1930. Her novels (such as, *The Age of Innocence*) were popular; however, Austen's women's stories ended more happily than Wharton's novels.

Female Scientists

There were many American women in the nineteenth century that make their mark in science: Sarah Frances Whiting (1846–1927), astronomer and physicist, Anna Winlock (1857–1904), an astronomer, Cornelia Clapp (1849–1934) a zoologist and Alice Evans (1881–1975), an American microbiologist. Other global notable women include: Maria Meurdrae, (1610–1680) who was a French chemist and alchemist; Genevieve Thiroux d'Arconville (1720–1805); Caterina Scarpellini (1808–1873) who was an Italian Astronomer; Anna Atkins (1700–1871), a well-known British botanist; and, Emmy Noether (1882–1935), a renowned German mathematician and physicist (symmetries and conservation laws) whom Einstein claimed to be a brilliant scientist. These women are all contributors to our society and well-being and we hope someday they and others will get their just recognitions for their accomplishments in their fields. We hope that the alleged women's museum in Washington DC gets approval for completion, since we do not hear about these female powerful leaders of the world in our current textbooks or courses.

Female Artists

Female artists have affected our culture and heritage in their wonderful work as painters. Art is the mirror of our souls and hearts as humans on this earth. Mary Cassatt (1844–1926) was a well-known impressionist painter who depicted social and family scenes. Her paintings of the intimacy of a mother and her child were poignant. Other painters include the wife of the Mexican painter Diego, Frida Kahlo, a surrealist painter who depicted in her work the cultural Mexican tradition and struggles in life and her work. Georgia O'Keeffe was married to Alfred Stieglitz (famous American photographer). She was a leading artist of the early twentieth century and her museum in Santa Fe is still regarded as extraordinary. Georgia captured the essence of the dessert and American west in her graphic natural mountain views and flowers. Her museum in New Mexico represents her notion of simplicity and the meaning of life.

Female University Pioneers

Women in the modern era started making great strides to make their mark in a man's world. There were many renowned female college graduates, such as Leta Hollingworth (1886–1939), who graduated with her doctorate from Columbia University majoring in psychology in 1916. She studied challenged students and coined the term "gifted" for her studies on children with IQs over 180. She provided support and managed several longitudinal studies over many years incorporating her ideas and educational strategies to help them achieve well in school and later in life. Elizabeth Blackwell (1821–1910) was the first American physician and graduated Genova Medical College. She was a doctor, and a public health activist who created a medical school for women in the 1860s. The twentieth century witnessed many more female college graduates who made their mark on history.

One of the first female physicians in Italy was Maria Montessori (1870–1952) known for scientific writings and educational philosophy that revolutionized teaching methods around the globe. She is the founder of the Montessori Method of education which is used today in many public and private schools world-wide. She was nominated several times for the Nobel Peace Prize; however, she did not win. Her work was widely accepted and proven to help children with learning disabilities. She created an environment that was safe for students, interacting with nature, animals, gardens and also highly creative for children to express their talents. She graduated from the University in Rome in 1896 as a doctor of medicine; however she was ridiculed and harassed during most of her courses. She studies several languages and travelled extensively and lived in India for some time. She lectured about her teaching method, writing several books and started schools wherever she visited around the world.

··

PART II

WOMEN LEADERS OF THE MODERN ERA

"IF A COUNTRY DOESN'T RECOGNIZE MINORITY RIGHTS
AND HUMAN RIGHTS, INCLUDING WOMEN'S RIGHTS, YOU
WILL NOT HAVE THE KIND OF STABILITY AND PROSPERITY
THAT IS POSSIBLE."

—Hillary Clinton

Historical books and biographies have enumerated many male heroes. We are beginning to acknowledge our female role models. Women are speaking about the need of the proposed National Women's History Museum (NWHM) in Washington. The founders of NWHM the are lobbying to have this museum approved by the senate. It was approved by the House of Representatives. It is surprising how much lobbying by female representatives had to occur to even

consider a special women's museum. We hope this legislature passes
and we encourage all to become members to support this enterprise.

Great Female Leaders

It is essentially that we continually speak out and provide a forum
to discuss issues that hold women back from reaching their own
potential as leaders in our global economy. Gender is not an issue if
people look at female leaders for what they stand for and their accomplishments. The following female leaders—in politics, business and
society, the arts and literature—are but a handful of those who have
changed our outlook and made our world a better place.

- *Sheryl Sandberg*—Sheryl wrote the book *Lean In: Women,
  Work, and the Will to Lead* to describe the lack of female
  leadership ambition in corporations. Women are capable of
  great leadership and need to take charge of their careers. She
  served as the chief operating officer of Facebook. Our culture
  applauds male accomplishments, whereas those of females
  are deemed worrisome. Sandberg is also spearheading a
  group of celebrities promoting a campaign to ban the word
  "*bossy*" in describing women leaders who take charge. The
  imagery of dominant males is much more acceptable in
  society; however, her courage to speak out is now a new
  example for all powerful women.

- *Oprah Winfrey*—Orpah is one of the wealthiest women
  in the world, rising from poverty through education into

broadcasting. She spent years hosting her own TV talk show and is the chair and CEO of HARPO Productions and chair (CEO/ CCO) of the Oprah Winfrey Network. She is an educator, humanitarian, and philanthropist who started girls' schools in Africa. She is author, producer, and actress of many films depicting the plight of black Americans. She has increased our literacy and reading capacity by endorsing many novels and self-help books. She is considered one of the most influential people in the world and in 2013 was awarded the Presidential Medal of Freedom.

- *Coco Chanel*—Coco revolutionized women's dress during the pre-WWI years from 1910 until 1913. She was an innovative designer of women's clothing using jersey (used for men's underwear) and getting rid of the corset. She developed the simple black dress and championed costume jewelry such as, a string of pearls. Her hat designs excluded bird plumage and were very simple highlighting the intrinsic worth of women. She supported the independent spirit of women-as-individuals in her fashion styles. She was independent and never married. Her vision and freedom for women were ahead of her time and endure to this day.

- *Debora L.* Spar—Debora is president of Barnard College, vocal advocate for women's leadership, and has written books on political economy, market rules, and how firms or government shape an evolving global economy. She taught courses in Harvard on politics of international business and economic development. Her latest book, *Wonder Women: Sex, Power and the Quest for Perfection,* discusses work/family balance issues. Debora started the Athena Center for Leadership Studies at Barnard and a global symposium for high-profile female leaders held each year in different regions of the world. Her work in women's leadership is never-ending and we commend her example.

- *Betty Friedan*—Betty was the first American woman in modern literature to expose the issues of women being second-class citizens. She stated women had *"no name"* and she published the *Feminine Mystique* in 1963. She spent years working to enact the Equal Rights Amendment, and became the first president of NOW (National Organization of Women). She spearheaded many activist movements that gave equal rights to women, especially equal pay and equal opportunity for higher-paying jobs. Her book remains widely read and still affects our society's attitudes towards women. Her ideals and reality of the plight of women is still quite powerful. We feel her written effect today.

- *Ariana Huffington*—Ariana is editor-in-chief of the digital media enterprise *Huffington Post.* She won a Pulitzer Prize in 2012 for its extraordinary online reporting capabilities. Her incredible journalistic talent has affected our modern political dialogue. She has been supportive of female leadership and continues to discuss issues in the global arena. Her stories are discussed in the media and create much debate. Ariana is innovative in her writing style, truthful in

her speeches, and outspoken for the rights of women. Her
online newspaper reaches millions; she has great influence
in our political arena. The *Huffington Post* impacts our daily
news and political ideals.

- *Indra Nooyi*—Indra is an American business executive of
PepsiCo, Inc. born in 1955 in India. She became the CEO of
PepsiCo, in 2006, and also the chair of the board in 2008. She
has revolutionized the soft drink and snack food industry
by introducing healthy snacks and diversifying products to
give the American public alternative choices. She has high
ethical, moral, and noble attributes that give her an edge in
the corporate world. She calls herself *brutally honest* which
only enhances her leadership capabilities and places great
emphasis on corporate values to keep her ship *unsinkable*.
Since assuming her position, she ranks in the top 10 Forbes
100 most powerful women.

- *Coretta Scott King*—Coretta (1927–2006) is considered the
"First Lady of Civil Rights". She has been involved in the civil
rights movement despite the wishes of her husband Martin
Luther King Jr. who wanted her to stay at home with the
children. She is an author, activist, civil rights leader and
started being very active in her own right in the 1960s. She
was a fantastic public speaker and liaison to the international
peace and justice organizations. Coretta was an international
peace ambassador and was revered by many countries. Her
message was one of peace and economic justice. She revered

Gandhi and she was a symbol for the struggle of human liberation from racism, and all forms of oppression.

The above women are only a few since there are many others,
which our history books and media have failed to cover, with accomplishments and policies. Our western culture has had some heroic
women such as, Amelia Earhart (1897–1937) in the 1930s. Her daring
flights made headlines providing young girls with a courageous role
model. Earhart said: "*Women must try to do things as men have tried.
When they fail their failure must be but a challenge to others.*" Great
leaders need to be aware of boundaries of self in doing deeds and in
relationships. Their heroism and bravery will shine in the shadows.
We acknowledge our female heroes.

A well-known French woman, Simone de Bouvoir (colleague of
Jean Paul Sartre) wrote *The Second Sex* in 1949 and laid the groundwork for many of the feminists that came after her published research.
She quoted Napoleon who stated "*a laughing woman was a conquered
woman*". Simone was outspoken in her day to discuss women's
oppression and suppression. Her book is still viable today since it is
comprehensive. A swedish author, Selma Lagerlof (1858–1940) was
the first female in 1909 to receive the Nobel Literature Prize.

Esther Perel is a contemporary author and lecturer on erotic intelligence that has changed male and female perceptions on how to keep
love energy alive in marriages and partnerships. She wrote, *Mating
in Captivity*, which is revolutionizing the ability of women to speak
out and talk about their needs using the five verbs: "*Ask, Give, Take,
Receive and Refuse*". She is known all over the globe for her outspoken

theories. Esther is truthful about women's sexual rights and gives them guidance to ask for their individual needs in their relationships with their partners. Women's power is realized through communication and women must find a new voice to express their needs.

Women with Courage

Our news is dotted with women making their mark in business and society. For example, Gloria Steinem, who is a spokesperson for equal rights for women and considered to be a world renowned feminist author, continues to cite the inadequacies of women in the modern era. She continues to point out how we objectify women and keep them subservient by not giving them equal opportunities and by not paying them equivalent wages as men. Our society continues to focus on gender inequalities and labeling, such as, "bossy." We cite the latest battles of Sheryl Sandberg with her book *Lean In* and others such as, Debora Spar, who supports and encourages female leadership, or female CEO's who made it up the ladder. They are all making their mark by cracking the glass ceiling of the "old boys'" network which kept women away from the board rooms. Women leaders need to encourage all women to speak up.

There are many women leaders in entertainment and the arts. Ida Lupino was one of the first female directors in our American film industry in the genre of film noir. Her films stand the test of time. Barbara Stanwyck was a key role model in the forties and fifties with her tough, strong, and independent spirit that inspired many women. Lucille Ball (in partnership with her husband, Desi Arnaz) was one of the first female producers in the 1950s. Later she ran the company by herself successfully. Other great female film stars such as, Marilyn Monroe and Natalie Wood were subject to male dominance and when trying to escape were caught in their crossfire. Joan Crawford was an independent actress and quite powerful in her dealings with Hollywood. She married Al Steele, the president of PepsiCo and after his death was voted into the Board of Directors in charge of publicity. She was an innovative and very independent female force in the acting world, and ultimately in the business world.

Currently since the large Hollywood studio contract system was abandoned in the 1950s many stars, male and female have their own production companies but before the 1950s women who broke apart were great stars such as, Katharine Hepburn, and Greta Garbo. There are also many female corporate leaders who accomplished great things in their high level executive offices. They came and went while cracking the glass ceiling. The system is different now and many actors have their own production companies. Women have to find clear goals with views on what they want and to not let fear stop them. Women are brilliant and if they have belief and opportunity they can succeed and become great leaders. Women leaders must support other women leaders, and then, we can empower each other.

Powerful Political Women

When corporate America was trying to keep women out of the board room we heard stories of African tribes who would have men heads of state but when emergencies arose they elected women to save them. Great female leaders have to be better than their male counterparts, such as not being late but always punctual, always ready with an agenda and on target with goals. Women had to be ten times better than their male counterparts in the same job to prove they could be given a chance to do the job; therefore, they developed incredible skills where we can see the results. Hillary Clinton said, *"What we have to do is to find a way to celebrate our diversity and debate our differences without fracturing our communities."* With such motivation and focus, women have accomplished a great deal. They had to speak their minds in the political arena and many people listened since they were powerful, outspoken and truthful. True leaders have authenticity and boundaries. They epitomize true essential leadership.

There are also other great leaders and we will review the most prominent political leaders. These are brave women who will face much debate and criticism since they are willing to speak out and take on the prejudice of our society. We also note the former prime minister of Britain, Margaret Thatcher who was dominant of conservative ideology during the eighties. Margaret Thatcher (free enterprise ideals) won wars for Britain to keep the Falkland Islands. She was the first female prime minister of England and ruled during the reign of Ronald Reagan. They both strategized a conservative form of government which we have had to deal with today. Hillary Clinton ran for the presidential nomination representing her party. One of the books she wrote, *It Takes a Village*, was well received with her vision for our children in America. We hope she continues her quest without prejudice. She has met several obstacles and gender bias. We wish all women equal opportunity to meet their goals.

Some great leaders met misfortunates in their careers. Indira Gandhi was India's third prime minister serving from 1966 to 1984, when she was assassinated. Benazir Bhutto was the first female prime minister of Pakistan in 1988 and was killed in 2007.Other female leaders are currently making their mark. Isabel Peron (born 1931) is a former president of Argentina and was the first non-royal female head of state in the Western hemisphere. Argentina has another female president called, Christina Fernandez de Kirchner sworn in for a second term in December 2011.

The following are some of the current powerful political women around the globe:

- *Christine Lagarde*—Christine is the French finance minister and the head of the International Monetary Fund (IMF) located in Belgium. She was instrumental in getting the European and American communities to work together for the good of the whole. Her speeches challenge the "BIG BOYS" since she urges immediate action to change the financial crisis. She is brave and is not afraid to tell it like it is; she speaks the truth. Christine is talented in the political arena to find solutions to global monetary dilemmas.

- *Angela Merkel*—Angela is the Chancellor of Germany in one of the most influential positions in the world. She is first female Chancellor and topped *Forbes* list—100 most powerful women in 2006–7. She was also one of the architects of the European Union. She is considered a very talented and powerful leader as a key player in the global economy. She not only influences other key players, but also manages to maintain a calm demeanor and an air of gravitas.

- *Gro Harlem Brundtland*—Gro is the prime minister of
  Norway and director of the World Health Organization.
  She is a doctor and is currently a global health leader. Her
  work is important for the international arena and she has
  improved Norway's economic status, as well as their tourist
  income with modern access to the fjords. She has influenced
  the economy of Norway and the health of the world with
  her innovative programs to make it attractive for people
  to contribute their support.

- *Michelle Bacheler*—Michelle is former president and defense
  minister of Chile and is now head of United Nations Women.
  Her work is groundbreaking for Chile who is now rising to
  great economic success. Her ground breaking women's
  programs have helped women's global status. Chile is gaining
  in the political arena since it is considered one of the richest
  countries in South America behind Brazil. Michelle is
  gaining popularity as one of the top female leaders.

- *Ellen Johsom-Sirleaf*—Ellen is President of Liberia and she
  is responsible for debt relief and investigating civil war
  crimes. Despite Liberia's violent history, she seems to be
  bringing some stability. Her belief for peace is making a
  difference. Her dedication to fighting for justice in her
  country has helped the world view her work and dedication
  as a beacon of light in the darkness.

- *Aung San Suu Kyi*—Once a prominent political prisoner in
  Burma (now known as Myanmar), Suu Kyi was the founder/
  chairperson of the National League for Democracy, fighting

against military rule and calling for her country's freedom.
A prisoner for 15 years, she won the Nobel Peace Prize in
1991. She continues her nonviolent resistance and gains
political followers who continue her work. Her fight is
an example for many other countries in the same plight.
Suu Kyi gives hope to all.

Currently the Eastern and Western hemispheres have had more
female rulers than our history tells and hopefully this will change in
the future as we gain confidence in our female leaders. Many female
leaders have always reiterated that the major problem they have is
balancing their work and family obligations; however, as the future
continues to support male/female caretakers, ease in making choices
will become more of a reality. Both men and women have to make
balanced choices and if done, fairly, they will succeed. History has
depicted great female leaders in a world which promoted freedom for
all people. Both men and women have changed our world for the better
through their dedication, hard work, and accomplishments. Imagine
what we can do together, as males and females working harmoniously.

Women in the Twentieth Century

In the modern era, other countries are more advanced than the
USA in female political leadership; however, these countries had
great male and female leaders. For example, England had Winston
Churchill and Margaret Thatcher. India had Mahatma Gandhi and
Indira Gandhi. Israel had Golda Meir and David Ben-Gurion. Many

Indonesian, African, and Asian nations have also elected females as heads of state. America needs to catch up and, hopefully, this can be accomplished in our lifetime. The following have been powerful women in our era:

- **Eleanor Roosevelt**—Eleanor changed the role of First Lady (1933–1945) as she took over many projects that her husband could not do. She also organized and joined prominent women's organization. In the face of criticism, she symbolized the quintessential independent and political woman of the last century. She was known for her work in the women's suffrage movement and the plight of the poor. She was an advocate for both civil and human rights and gave effective speeches. Women's issues as gender commodities were also disclosed.

- **Queen Elizabeth II**—The Queen is noted for her ability to persevere and loyalty for England for more than 60 years of reigning. She has seen and been involved in all of the modern era events after WWII. Her constancy and intelligent leadership has inspired many to do their best and be ready for changes with her great adaptive skills. The Queen continues to be steadfast in her ruling and has become a symbol of loyalty and peace throughout the world.

- **Hillary Clinton**—Hillary was a former senator of New York and U.S. secretary of State. She was also former First Lady. She helped reform many policies in her political career and she is considered one of the most brilliant females in politics.

As Secretary of State, she accomplished many strategic goals for our foreign policy. She was active as First Lady and has an exceptional political savvy. She is a likely candidate for the presidency; however, she is not alone since many qualified women are also in the political scene. She has written many books on her experiences.

Several women made their mark in history and made a difference in our country, such as Oprah Winfrey who not only built a massive TV empire but also schools for children in Africa. She started a girls' education center which places an emphasis on young girls who are subject to tyranny. Oprah's mentor was the renowned poet and author Maya Angelou, who also was an advocate for women's civil rights and wrote about the freedom to sing their song. They both were dedicated to improving our physical, emotion and mental well-being. Oprah is still very active in promoting the arts, books, exercise and the pursuit of a healthy lifestyle.

Great Female Scientists

We know that science was not a popular choice or subject for many young women attending college. We remember that young women were not expected to do well in math and science and these roles were always expected of their male counterparts. Things have changed and we now have a great increase of women doctors, scientists, and engineers. Their contribution in these fields have been astronomical and we continue to praise their accomplishments. We know that our culture promoted male scientists and yet the world has produced some of the best female scientists who have gained prominence all over the globe. We listed a few below:

- *Madame Curie*—Marie Curie (1867–1934) was Polish and became a naturalized French physicist and chemist, discovering radium and polonium in 1898. She won worldwide fame in the early 1900s. Although she started with her husband, she became the sole researcher of her work. Her pioneering research in radiation, which earned her one of her two Nobel Prizes, led directly to her death at 67; nevertheless, her search for truth never wavered. Her work encouraged many young women to become scientists since she was fearless in the world dominated scientific world. Madame Curie was one of a kind and is unforgettable. She continues to be a role model for many female children.

- *Jane Goodall*—Jane is a British author and anthropologist born in 1934 spending most of her life studying chimpanzees in Tanzania, Africa. Her recent engagements all over the world reiterate the need for environmental protocol to curtail global warming and the killing of animals in Africa. Her book, *Reason for Hope: A Spiritual Journey,* describes the environmental dangers our world is heading for and the societal mores of primitive animals. She noted the close supportive and affectionate bonds in family and social relationships of chimpanzees; however, she also reported on their brutal

and aggressive action for status in society. We learned a lot
about our behavior from her research.

- *Francoise Barre-Sinoussi*—Francoise was born in 1947 and
  is a French virologist and director of the Regulation of
  Retroviral Infections Division at the *Institut Pasteur* in Paris,
  France. She studied retroviruses and in 1983 discovered HIV.
  She received the Nobel Prize in 2008 sharing it with her
  mentor Harold zur Hausen who discovered and developed
  the cervical cancer vaccine. Barre-Sinoussi continues to work
  with developing countries to improve the treatment for and
  prevent the spread of HIV/AIDS. Her work is regarded as
  critical for the survival of AIDS patients. She also studies the
  adaptive immune response to viruses. There are many health
  organizations grateful for her work.

- *Rachel Carson*—Rachel (1907–1964) was a well-known
  American author, marine biologist and environmentalist.
  She was as astute and ethical conservationist whose book
  Silent Spring advanced the global environmental movement.
  She was an ecologist, and advocate for nature whose books
  changed the world. Rachel worked for the U.S. Bureau of
  Fisheries and was instrumental in our banning the use
  of many pesticides. She wrote a trilogy: *The Sea Around Us,
  The Edge of the Sea, and Under the Sea Wind.* Also
  published was a well-known biography for children
  explaining the benefits of exploring the sea edge. There is
  a Rachel Carson National Wildlife Refuge in Maine.

- *Margaret Mead*—A well-known American cultural anthropologist (1901–1978) and author who spoke to nation-wide audiences in the '60s and '70s bringing awareness to the debate of nature vs. nurture. Her work involved extensive studies on cultures all over the world (Samoa, New Guinea, etc.), describing human behavior, mores and societal expectations. Her books described adolescent conflicts due to nature versus civilization (*Coming of Age in Samoa*, written in 1928) and three primitive societies depicting how social attitudes affect sex differences (*Sex and Temperament in Three Primitive Societies*, written in 1935).

- *Grace Hopper* (1906–1992)—A computer scientist and U.S. Navy rear admiral, in 1959 Hopper designed *COBOL* (*CO*mmon *B*usiness *O*riented *L*anguage), which revolutionized corporate finance and administrative systems by introducing a simple programming language for large computers. Her brilliant system and its technical design made it easy for programmers to fix glitches. Prior to her invention, programming was difficult and time consuming. COBOL made it easier and women were hired to do the job. Modern business technology is the direct result of her innovations.

- *Tania Singer*—Tania, a German professor of neuroscience, was born in 1969 and is the director of the department of social neuroscience at the Max Plank Institute (Human Cognitive and Brain Sciences). She received her PhD in psychology in Berlin and her research focuses on developmental, neuronal and hormonal mechanisms underlying social behavior, especially the social moral emotions such as, empathy, compassion, envy and fairness. She investigates the roles of cooperation, social decision-making and neural communication. Dr. Singer studies cooperative and prosocial behavior versus selfish behavior. Her work is groundbreaking and she is considered a world expert on empathy and pain.

There have been countless powerful women through the ages, and no single list—no matter how exhaustive an attempt—can possibly do them all justice. There is much to do in our world, and those we *have* mentioned continually inspire us to tackle the greatest inequities and injustices. We look forward to a future society of great and powerful women who are encouraged to fulfill their potential with the support of a society that recognizes their worth.

PART III

....

GLOBAL FEMALE LEADERS

"LEADERSHIP IS HARD TO DEFINE AND GOOD LEADERSHIP
EVEN HARDER. BUT IF YOU CAN GET PEOPLE TO FOLLOW YOU
TO THE ENDS OF THE EARTH, YOU ARE A GOOD LEADER."

—Indra Nooyi

Great leaders are secure as strong individuals with a vision and
purpose. We need to develop our young children to feel competent
and able to lead and accomplish great things. Our world must provide a platform them. Young women feel they have to count, work,
and deserve recognition; they need to express themselves and have
confidence and self-esteem. The future is in their hands. They need
role models and mentors. We are ready for them to come together to
work with male counterparts. Our country may be only 238 years old;
however, now we can readily receive great female leaders. America

61

is waiting; however, women must "stick together" to support and give each other chances to succeed. They must realize their female potential and not sabotage themselves or each other. We are waiting with bated breath.

During the era around 500 BC and before, five major countries revered their female citizens and they were given at least some equal rights: Ancient Greece, Mesopotamia, Phoenicia, Etruscans, and the territories of the Celts. In summary, there were many female leaders before the Roman Empire and then again during the middle ages. In between female leaders were part of the church and the nunnery where they had freedom to learn and become educated. In ancient Rome after the republic began (at the beginning of the new era after Christ) there were "*five good emperors*". Marcus Aurelius was the last of them (121–180 AD) and ruled Rome from 161–180 AD; a great stoic philosopher, poet, benevolent ruler, he wrote books, the most notable of which was *Meditations*. After this era, women had lost some of the power enjoyed by their predecessors. We speculate that wars motivated by empire-building and greed became the norm.

Emerging Powerful Queens

It seemed that, with the exception of Cleopatra, the Roman empire became male dominated; however, after the fall of Rome we have a bevy of European queens who emerged from the medieval times, such as Eleanor of Aquitaine (1122–1204), one of the wealthiest and powerful women in all of Western Europe during this time. She participated in the crusades in one of their adventures with the King of France. Following her regal status was Margaret the first, Queen of Denmark (Danish regent), who in 1389 united the monarchies of Denmark, Norway, and Sweden. Women emerged as powerful queen regents or consorts and ruled covertly if not overtly at times. As for the fifteenth century, we see many queen consorts, such as Joan of Navarre (queen of England until the death of her husband, Henry IV, in 1413) and others.

Beginning in the fifteenth century, Europe has seen many queens, but the three most powerful were:

1) Mary Queen of Scots, ruler of England and wife of the King of France (16th century),

2) Queen Elizabeth I of England and Ireland (16th century), and

3) Queen Kristina of Sweden (17th century), Goth (part of Germany), and Vandals (part of Poland).

They had their own conflicts, struggles for independence, and turbulence during their reigns. Mary the Queen of Scots was the only one who married and she had her problems including threats on her life during her reign. Most queens found themselves in the position of having to marry to produce an heir which was considered their main purpose and job. We know Queen Kristina of Sweden decided to abdicate to pursue other interests and gain her freedom.

We realize that Queen Kristina of Sweden had remarkable intelligence and studied previous kings or queens and their successes. They had to fight battles when protecting their realms and to claim freedom. She did not want to marry since she would lose what she had.

Mary Queen of Scots was manipulated by powerful men; however, she fought hard to reclaim the English throne that she thought was rightfully hers. Queen Kristina avoided marriage and was not good at manipulating her suitors to give her more power as Queen Elizabeth I did. Queen Kristina ended the 30 year war and was buried in the Vatican, side by side with cardinals and bishops, the only woman to do so. How did a Swedish Queen end up there? How did a Queen from a strict Lutheran Protestant country end up catholic? The following is a synopsis of her life which was depicted in Veronica Buckley's book, *Christina, Queen of Sweden: The Restless Life of a European Eccentric* written in 2004.

Queen Kristina's Story

Kristina was born to King Gustav Adolf and Queen Maria Elena. A son was expected but after three infant deaths, her father thanked God for the healthy daughter and promised that she would be just as important to him as a boy. Her dad Gustav II Adolf had for 21 years taken Sweden through many wars; however, he also adapted Sweden to the European community with its culture and education. It was a cold world since Europe experienced for hundreds of years the "Little Ice Age" with poverty and hunger. Women were supposed to bear children until they died. Kristina's dad died when she was 6 years old killed in a war. Kristina was a happy young queen, eager to learn. Her dad's friends, who had studied in universities in Uppsala, Sweden, Germany, Holland, France, and England, were her teachers.

She learned new languages, philosophy, law, medicine and scientific experimentation. Kristina loved to read about Caesar; her favorite hero was Alexander the Great, and would identify with his male bravery. She studied the strong and weak sides of Europe. She learned about Queen Elizabeth of England whom she admired, since she conquered the Spanish Armada 50 years earlier. Queen Elizabeth I, the Protestant Queen was known and admired in Sweden. Queen Elizabeth I had endured six years in prison during a very unstable time, and she still moved her country into the golden years with her intellect, great education in politics, and languages. Kristina was raised like a man, riding, hunting; she loved the outdoors, her horses, and dogs. The military was her major interest. At 18, she was officially the queen.

Kristina was pressed to get married which she never did. So she chose her cousin Karl Gustav to be her successor in case she would die. Karl Gustav was in love with Kristina and for many years believed that they would marry. Queen Kristina met the French King Louis XIV and created the guarantee for peace after 30 years of religious wars. She made Sweden the victor and got lots of gifts, land and art pieces which helped found the first National Art collection. The Russian Tsar Aleksey begged Sweden for peace. She was often ill and a French doctor changed her diet; he got her to exercise and bathe more.

Kristina corresponded with the philosopher Descartes, who was Catholic and she would ask him questions like; "How do you fall in love with someone before you even know the person", *he would answer,* "probably there is something you see in that person that reminds you of someone you love". *She would ask:* "What is the difference between spiritual and passionate love; what is the worst: to abuse, to hate or to love?" *She forced Descartes to come to visit her in Sweden. He was the one that moved her from Lutheran to Catholicism.*

In October 1650, she was crowned Queen in Stockholm at 23 years old, with extravagance since Sweden had to express her authority. By 1654, she was ready to abdicate; not give up her title as queen but to make her cousin Karl Gustav, king and head of Sweden. Her reason was very scandalous; she was moving to Rome to be a catholic, an absolute treason. She secretly sent messages to the pope about her arriving.. Her cousin was crowned the same day and died after six years. Queen Kristina lived in Rome and died at the age of 62. Her indomitable spirit is alive and is a great example to all.

Modern Powerful Queens

Beginning in the eighteenth century, Europe began the modern era with three powerful queens:

1) Catherine the Great, queen and empress of all the Russias (18th century),
2) Queen Victoria of Great Britian and including her great empire around the world (19th century), and
3) Queen Elizabeth II of the United Kingdom and the Commonwealth (20th-21st century).

The queens of Europe from the 16th to the 21st centuries span 500 years of powerful female leaders. We are 230 years young; however we have not began our journey of female heads of state.

Global Female Scientists

In history, we acknowledge and see that there have been many women scientists. As children, we only had what the world offered for female role models. Margaret Mead made herself known with many lectures on her findings including: Personality traits such as masculine and feminine are not linked so much to sex but also to society. Many women have made their mark in science and we are grateful for their hard work, dedication and contributions. Movies were made on Madame Curie which helped convey the effect she had on the future of our world. Madame Curie was the most well-known female scientist at the beginning of the modern era. She led the pack by becoming the quintessential role model, not only for her family but also, for the world. She won her first Nobel Prize in 1903 (for Physics) and a second one (for Chemistry) in 1911. Several other female scientists have followed in her footsteps.

Female Science Nobel Prize Winners

Recipient	Shared	Year	Prize
Irene Joliot Curie (Madame Curie's daughter)	her husband Jean Frederic Joliot	1935	Chemistry
Gerty Theresa Cori, née Radnitz		1947	Physiology or Medicine
Maria Goeppert-Mayer	Hans D. Jensen and Eugene Paul Wigner	1963	Physics

Recipient	Shared	Year	Prize
Dorothy Crowfoot Hodgkin		1964	Chemistry
Rosalyn Sussman Yalow		1977	Physiology or Medicine
Barbara McClintock		1983	Physiology or Medicine
Rita Levi-Montalcini		1986	Physiology or Medicine
Gertrude B. Elion	Sir James W. Black	1988	Physiology or Medicine
Christiane Nüsslein-Volhard		1995	Physiology or Medicine
Linda B. Buck American neuroscientist		2004	Physiology or Medicine
Françoise Barré-Sinoussi French virologist and immunity diseases	Luc Montagnier and Harald zur Hausen	2008	Physiology or Medicine
Ada E. Yonath		2009	Chemistry
Elizabeth H. Blackburn & Carol W. Greider	Jack. W. Szostak	2009	Physiology or Medicine

Peace and Literature Nobel Prize Winners

Women have contributed to our global peace concerns and also have been recognized in the field of literature. We acknowledge these Nobel Prize Award–winning women:

Recipient	Shared With	Year	Prize
Baroness von Suttner, "Countess Kinsky"		1905	Peace
Jane Addams		1931	Peace
Emily Greene Balch		1946	Peace
Betty Williams	Mairead Corrigan	1976	Peace
Mother Teresa		1979	Peace
Alva Myrdal		1982	Peace
Aung San Suu Kyi		1991	Peace
Rigoberta Menchu Tum		1992	Peace
Jody Williams		1997	Peace
Shirin Ebadi		2003	Peace
Wangari Muta Maathai		2004	Peace
Tawakkol Karman	Leymah Gbowee, Ellen Johnson Sirleaf	2011	Peace
Selma Lageriof		1909	Literature
Grazia Deledda		1926	Literature
Sigird Undset		1928	Literature
Pearl Buck		1938	Literature
Gabriela Mistral		1945	Literature
Nelly Sachs	Shmuel Agnon	1966	Literature
Nadine Gordimer		1991	Literature
Toni Morrison		1993	Literature
Wislawa Szymborska		1996	Literature

Recipient	Shared With	Year	Prize
Elfriede Jelinek		2004	Literature
Doris Lessing		2007	Literature
Herta Muller		2009	Literature
Alice Munro		2013	Literature

Attributes of Women Leaders

Being a female leader in any capacity has not only great responsibilities, but also, character behavior that must be followed to be successful. Great leaders are courageous and fearless since they take risks without worrying if they did something wrong. They trust their own judgment and have confidence in their decisions. Their confidence and vision inspires other to be courageous and noble in their acts. They do not judge others but listen and respect their views. As Matthew 7:3 states, *"Do not judge others lest you be judged the same way."* Even when we do judge others, we do not have to act on those judgments.

Great leaders have visions that can be projected for others to follow and do not haggle with little judgmental actions that are not productive but create chaos and smoke. They feel willing to take on responsibilities that benefit those who follow their guidance. Great leaders are not busy with putting other people down or judging their actions, since their time or energy is focused on getting the job done. They are the examples for others to follow and learn from so that they can become leaders when it is their time. Female leaders need to develop programs for our youth and young girls need role models for them to imagine other possibilities.

Leadership Without Judgment

Great leaders have no time to spend on judging others since solutions of real problems takes precedence. Authentic leaders see the truth within each person and know that to judge others creates distractions and gossip avoiding finding solutions. Judging others hinders great creativity. Ideas must flow freely. Clear boundaries keep leaders from judging and taking things personally. Separating your ego from what is happening in a chaotic or dramatic environment allows you to make clear decisions that are relevant to the situation. Judgment is required when making decisions or discriminating new ideas and when determining correct choices. Discernment is a skill; being a separate and total individual helps you avoid busy and unproductive behavior and work.

People who judge others are misusing their time; they use judgments as a way to procrastinate and not focus on what is important. Judgments cloud the issues, and preclude solutions. Many state institutions are known for bureaucratic mayhem that cloud problems and, therefore, preclude any solutions. They create chaos to control situations. We need to be authentic, productive, and nonjudgmental of others to work well. Female leaders working with male leaders can help clear the way for bona fide solutions. We can support each other and be on the same team. We can work together for the benefit of humanity, the world, and for global interactions.

ABOUT THE INTERVIEWEE

DIANA T. VAGELOS

We interviewed men and women who know what makes a great leader and who have themselves developed the attributes, personalities, and vision that lead to success. Seven questions gave some structure to the interviews; however, we allowed the interviewee the freedom to discuss what they felt was important.

Diana Touliatou Vagelos is a well-known humanitarian, patron of the arts, entrepreneur, and philanthropist. She is dedicated to the education of women and helps guide several service and policy-making organizations that promote high ideals and civil goals. As a student of Barnard College, Diana Vagelos was an economics major and a scholarship student for four years. At graduation she was selected by her classmates to receive the Frank Gilbert Bryson Prize for contributing the most to the college's life while a student. Mrs. Vagelos has served as a Trustee of Barnard college intermittently since 1991 and is presently Vice-Chair of the Board. In 2010, Diana and her husband, Dr. Roy P. Vagelos, were major donors to Barnard for the completion of "The Diana Center", an architectural wonder used by students for social and intellectual gatherings, cultural endeavors, and performing arts.

Diana served on the Board of Directors of the New Jersey Performing Arts Center and was long term Chair of its Arts Education Committee. She was also a founding member of the Women's Association of NJPAC and served as its first president. Mrs. Vagelos is also engaged in many innovative endeavors such as, helping the New Jersey Performing Arts Center continue its development and serving on the board of WNET Channel 13, New York City's PBS station.

In May 2012, Diana received The Women's City Club of New York's *Civic Spirit Award* for her leadership. The Women's City Club is a nonprofit organization of 600 volunteer members that has spent 99 years dedicated to city issues, social responsibility, and the civil needs of the community. The club addresses vital causes that matter most for New Yorkers, tackling legislative and regulatory changes as needed. Through her work, Diana Vagelos represents the quintessential noble woman, educating New Yorkers to be the leaders for changes, and policy improvements. Her communication skills, sincerity, generosity, and warm personality are treasures for all to enjoy when fortunate to be in her presence.

1. What axiom do you feel is the secret to your success, the most important mantra in keeping your leadership unique?

One of the most important things a leader has to do, regardless of the group or project, as well as where or what you are doing, is to "listen to the group". If you are going to lead, it is imperative to listen, or else there will be no connection, no effect. Find out who the people in the group are, what their goals and aspirations are, as well as what causes them anxiety. You have to know what they consider are "real problems", otherwise you won't be able to really communicate with them. If you fail to listen, then you are only talking about your own issues, which are not really theirs. If you are going to be a leader, the group needs to be more important than you are. Narcissists like to talk about themselves; some people have a very big ego, some don't, but no one can forget himself or herself very easily. Listening and learning will never get you into trouble—but not listening will. One cannot control everything; experience teaches you how to identify the things you are able to control.

Society is now more mindful and more communicative. Today's media has a substantial impact on society's mindset. Listening means remaining open to everything; however, that can be complicated and distracting. Many things out there are not relevant to your issues—and yet the media brings it to your attention and you cannot help but hear about it. If we actually listen to everything, it's hard to focus on anything. You have to discern what's important; you have to trust and work as a team with a vision. This comes from the original direction: Listen. Once you listen and incorporate what you hear into additional strategies, people will follow your lead much more readily. If you listen, they can be reciprocal. You have to be reciprocal about all concerns; if you aren't, you will lose your following.

2. What accomplishments are you most proud to have been part of, and how did you achieve these successes?

I have been fortunate to be involved with many great organizations, and have even started a few from the ground up. I gained much of this experience through my work with the New Jersey Performing Arts Center (NJPAC) and the Women's City Club. As founder of the NJPAC, I had to formulate ground rules that would guide future members of the organization. I was able to build consensus among all participants—individuals from all walks of life. As founder, I also had to set the protocol and establish the business direction. We spent over a year on just the bylaws, which were probably the trickiest things—some people are interested, but bylaws are legalistic and many don't want to be bothered with it or spend time on the detail.

Every organization eventually must have guidelines, if it's going to grow. Guidelines are what the bylaws amount to; in a sense, they set the tone for the organization. Turnover, for example, is inevitable, so you must set appropriate terms. When people depart from an organization it must be decided what they are entitled to. The rules and protocol of the organization are set in the bylaws. You don't really want an organization to have the same leadership for the next 15 years, so it's a good idea to introduce in the bylaws the duration of the term. People—from the leadership down—need to have a sense of what to expect and the process of succession needs to be laid out. Bylaws prepare individuals and the organization itself for turnover. That's extremely important; it is part of your job to ensure your successor can easily adapt to and meet the requirements of the position.

This is the message we have sent early on. We believe that everyone in the organization has the right to know what the rules are and what the protocol is—everyone is very clear on the objectives. Bylaws are built into the system for turnaround and change. Without clear bylaws, people can interpret behavior to gain personal interest above the interest of the organization. Becoming clear in your role in the organization precludes any misinterpretations or disappointments. Leadership involves being able to handle change. Determine the intentions of your organization's new blood, and ensure they are able to adapt to change.

3. How would you describe your relationships with your closest colleagues, and with the people that you depended on to get the job done?

As far as colleges are concerned there are two different types of people involved, the ones that get paid and the ones that volunteer. As a volunteer you are in the unusual position of having to work with staff members for whom this is a paid job. You must adapt to fit in because this is their livelihood and they are evaluated for their work. It will benefit you to be personally involved with the staff—they have the institutional knowledge and know what's required. You are not there to give them work to do; you're there to work with them as a team and to get everyone involved. Remember that most people want to feel like they are making a contribution to something important. Making suggestions built on collaboration is one way to approach and appeal to new people: "If we could reach out quickly in this way, I would be very happy to initiate the calls and keep things moving." You'll find that people will engage faster and be happier with the process. If you are an outsider, this effort will immediately make you less of one, and you will begin to be accepted as part of the team.

4. How did you deal with stress and how did you handle conflicts with your team members?

Being a volunteer immediately lowers the stress level—you're not being paid and you have no fear of losing your job. But whether you are a volunteer or a staff person, everyone is always judging everybody a little bit.

It's definitely less stressful if you are open to criticism. You not only have to be very careful of how you offer criticism but also very resilient when receiving criticism. Don't take it personally; instead, take a moment to consider whether the criticism is reasonable or not. Criticism and stress often go together, but you must not allow it to prevent you from being positive. I have never been in a situation where the criticism or stress has prevented me from being positive or constructive. In the face of reasonable criticism, you must reorganize, regroup, and start fresh. Be sure you don't blindside anyone with any changes; no one likes to be shocked or unprepared. This is all a part of dealing with people. You want people to work together and achieve a common goal. If you routinely shock them and make them uncomfortable, they will not stay around long.

5. How would you describe your career stages, and what were the major turning points that helped you reach your highest level?

I never really had a career in the traditional sense. I didn't want the restrictions required, because I was raising four children, which was quite time-consuming. My circumstances required me to avoid the time restrictions of working full-time in an organization. I needed flexibility for each child because I had to be able to adapt and react to their needs. Some people can do it all and don't need flexibility. It's easier, of course, if you have a family member living with you who helps take care of children. So even though I never went through stages and turning points myself, I've been involved with many organizations that have experienced significant change.

My highest level of work involved drafting bylaws in new organizations to provide growth, vision, and new direction. These bylaws need to be firm, yet flexible, capable of being updated to reflect the relationships in the company. You must be able to readily adapt to these relationships in order to succeed. You don't want anything written in stone. There are two kinds of leaders: those who can adapt and handle change, and those who cannot. *Those who cannot adapt will disappear. Leaders have to lead through changes within the organization.*

I have had the privilege of serving on the boards of Barnard College, NJPAC, and WNET. When you join an organization that is already formed you must learn everything you can about it and look for cracks. I continue to expand my knowledge of each organization's business by listening to its current leaders. WNET is one of the few channels to produce programs that I both enjoy watching and feel are worthwhile. What we are looking for is originality and something no one else has thought of or was interested in developing. If I did not support the station's goals, I could not be a part of this team—my contributions would be inauthentic. If you hide your true feelings and are superficial, it will be hard on you; however, even more important, you will fail as a member of that team. If you find there is something relevant that has not been addressed at this time, that's when you step in and work with others to make changes; this is the time you become a leader. If you see something missing or lacking, you must be willing to work for it. You have to think about it; have some ideas, and then make a plan.

6. What inspired you and how did you inspire the people who worked with you? How did people help you accomplish your goals, and how did you help them accomplish theirs?

In order to inspire others to work for you, you must have a vision—a plan to meet the needs and requirements of the organization. If you have a new idea for an organization, you really have to sell it. No one is likely to embrace the idea right away. To get others involved, you must be involved. If you just delegate the work to someone else and say, "I think you need to do this or that," you cannot simply expect them to embrace your vision. An authentic leader leads by example, but ensures others are part of any idea from its inception. People need to feel that they are an integral part of the organization and contributing to its growth. If they can't see the need for change, they may not be convinced until they see the benefit from your idea. Sometimes this requires experimentation; if you make a mistake, learn from it. If something conflicts with your view or vision, be flexible and adapt quickly.

7. What would you like to communicate about your leadership style, experience, or where you are now?

The biggest challenge for women who are married or raising a family is the balancing act between their home and work lives. The family dynamics have to be clear for everyone, especially when both spouses are working. Women have to make a conscious decision about the balancing act. If you want to become a leader in your organization, you must make sacrifices and long hours is one of them—you will not, for example, be going home at 5 p.m. The people who toil away at professions where they do not have a calling can throw in the towel; true leaders, however, must have a calling, and must make the necessary sacrifices to succeed in their profession.

My vision for the company that I started in New Jersey included an annual luncheon where original board members were always invited to attend. Bringing together past and present board members required courage; the city had endured significant problems for 20 years. But everyone involved wanted to attend this big fundraiser and help the organization succeed. My belief was that all board members, past and present, had helped shape an effective organization. Making something a little better is extremely worthwhile. If you find you can no longer improve an organization, that's the time to move on—it doesn't need you anymore. It may be fun to stay when you are in tune with an organization's goals, but you must find a reason to be there, and a niche in which you can be productive. I never seem to go too long without finding something to do or improvements to make. As time goes on, I am continually reminded there is always more to do. If you give up on doing things for your community and fellow man then life is over.

Section Two

Balancing the Divide

"You may not control all the events
that happen to you, but you can decide
not to be reduced by them."

"Courage is the most important of
all the virtues because without courage,
you cannot practice any other
virtue consistently."

"You cannot use up creativity.
The more you use, the more you have."

—MAYA ANGELOU

AMERICAN POET, AUTHOR

AND HUMAN RIGHTS ADVOCATE

Gender Leader Balance

Our country has acknowledged its male leaders throughout history; however, we cannot report that the same has been true for most female leaders. It is true that women of power have been recognized; however, we need to do more to balance the divide of male and female leaders. We know this is possible with great partnerships; females need recognition. For example, Emily Roebling was the secret architect/engineer of the Brooklyn Bridge completed in 1883 since she supervised the day to day operations for 11 years after taking over for her husband John who was incapacitated in 1872. She was an avid student of civil engineering and John trained and taught Emily higher mathematics (stress analysis, cable construction and catenary curves) to complete the job; the bridge is revered as an architectural wonder that still exists today. We have recently witnessed some evidence of gender-spanning success that changed our society in the fields of communications and technology, with a great leader representing each gender:

1) Oprah Winfrey (born 1954), who established a multimedia empire that distributes expert views on health and well-being; revolutionizing our ability to connect emotionally; Oprah is one of the most powerful women in the world; and,

2) Steve Jobs (1955–2011), who co-founded both Apple Computer and Pixar Animation Studios, revolutionizing human communications across music, media, and technology; his personality brought together the geniuses required to create a new world.

These two exemplary leaders represent extreme examples. All leaders face complex decisions every day, and the ability to incorporate diverse opinions from both genders can help drive those decisions. Colleagues and collaborators working together must first establish a common ground, a goal often made more elusive by the differences between men and women. Even though many same-sex partnerships manage to achieve success, we feel the best formula reflects a constructive combination of male and female personas.

The Male/Female Divide

We are all humans, first and foremost, yet gender always remains a critical, if secondary, consideration. Is there a great male/female divide? There are differences between individuals that have nothing to do with gender, but we must still acknowledge the chasm between male and female identity. The irrefutable fact is that our society has long suffered from a gender gap between males and females, with constant conflicts, biases, and challenges. Our American life of 238 years has seen this battle of the male/female divide for too long. Uniting the two genders requires us to reach across the ephemeral great divide, just as our ancestors built bridges to handle physical chasms. Our bridge is physical at first but must become spiritual.

We need to build bridges in order to achieve success, and bridges (connections) are important for all genders. Bridges are first built as physical edifices; however, our goal is to eventually have invisible bridges in the spiritual domain where gender cannot rule. The best bridge balances are products of compatible relationships. Building these bridges does not mean forcing only one side or the other completely from its comfort zone. Successful problem solving requires dedication; without focus and hard work, solutions can escape us.

The Bill and Melinda Gates Foundation, for example, is a philanthropic organization, founded by Bill, the Microsoft Corp. co-founder and his wife, Melinda. They help educate children and promote healthcare all over the world. The couple met at Microsoft and have been married for 20 years—a bridge-based relationship that has flourished. Approached properly, a bridge of that nature can enable us to reach a communal platform of understanding upon which we can meet, exchange ideas, and collaboratively solve problems. At times, men have to travel a bit further across the bridge; at other times, women do. In either case, we can meet in the middle of the great divide, eliminating the chasm in order to work together in creative, innovative, and dynamic ways. This can occur as we learn to balance our corporations and institutions.

PART IV

. . . .

MALE AND FEMALE DIFFERENCES

"VANITY AND PRIDE ARE DIFFERENT THINGS, THOUGH
THE WORDS ARE OFTEN USED SYNONYMOUSLY. A PERSON
MAY BE PROUD WITHOUT BEING VAIN. PRIDE RELATES MORE
TO OUR OPINION OF OURSELVES; VANITY, TO WHAT WE
WOULD HAVE OTHERS THINK OF US."

—Jane Austen

We become aware early on that males and females are different. Around age 2, young children begin to understand that they are "boys" or "girls"—and the drama begins. Society takes over and differences between female and male behavior are introduced. We know that, broadly speaking, there are gender-specific physical attributes; however, men and women all think and feel and talk. We all want to be loved and we all want to succeed. And this is hardly a zero-sum game; men need not fail in order for women to succeed. If we fear our differences then we're *all* sure to fail; only by working together can we conquer our problems, establish and maintain peace, discover a safe way to live, and survive as citizens of our common planet.

The fabric of society and the health of the environment depend on our ability to work together and solve problems. The world's very survival is at stake. Women must therefore take on leadership roles throughout the United States and beyond. Many women are equally or more capable—and some are equally or more experienced—than some men currently in those roles. Both men and women can make mistakes in leadership roles; however, we should not dwell and focus only on females who make mistakes in corporate or political undertakings. Understanding *how* men and women are different, and recognizing the flaws common to each, can help us develop ways of working together. We need balance within us and with others.

Realization of the Self

Understanding ourselves evolves with mindfulness and the ability to observe our own behavior. The psychoanalyst Carl Jung, who for some time worked with Sigmund Freud, argued that *self-realization* came from the integration of the many parts of self. Realization of self involves being aware of the parts of ourselves. Jung believed that the self has five major parts:

1) *The Persona* (provides the external mask of self), which resides in our conscious self and deals with the outside world; this refers to the part of ourselves that we present to others, such as our personality.

2) *The Ego* (protects the internal self), which resides on the cusp of the conscious and unconscious selves; this refers to the part of ourselves that tries to keep us honest with who we are and protects our real or true inner self.

3) *The Shadow* (feels bad and shameful), which resides in the unconscious self and contains the dark self; this refers to the part of ourselves that we have difficulty accepting since we may not approve of its thoughts or actions.

4) *The Anima/Animus* (represents female and male parts of self), which resides below the shadow; this refers to the part of ourselves that many do not acknowledge but is very real since we all are governed by our hormones and views of our strengths.

5) *The Self* (resides at the center of entire psyche), which is the essence of our true and real selves; this refers to the inner part of who we really are, considered by some to be our soul and requiring protection since it is vulnerable.

According to Murray Stein's book *Jung's Map of the Soul*, Jung stated that self-integration hinges on acceptance of the non-persona parts of self. You must deal with your *shadow* and *anima/animus* aspects before you can become self-realized—in touch with your real self—and self-realization is a prerequisite for becoming creative or great. Jung also believed that dealing with the shadow parts of self—the unknown aspects, which can sabotage your goals—required a great deal of courage. Most successful leaders have come to terms with their shadow part, but achieving *true* greatness requires them to deal with the anima/animus aspect of self as well. All great leaders have an energetic vitality—one that draws on the real internal self—that enables them to exhibit their courage, communicate their intention, and provide inspiration.

As described by Jung, the soul or true self is barricaded within the unconscious. The process of reaching it requires strength of character, bravery, analytical ability, balance of self, and the sheer determination to find one's own truth. Truly great leaders have accomplished some form of soul searching to become the best reflection of their respective eras and cultures. The terms *"ego* and *selfish"*, according to Stein, are misinterpreted: *"When the ego is well connected to the self, a person reaches his or her true essence without any narcissistic tendencies."*

When the ancient Greeks advised that a person, *"Know Thyself,"* they were referring to a process requiring years of self-observation and analysis. As a starting point, the following *5 Bs* will help you build bridges within the parts of self and thereby help you connect to others:

Relationship Attributes

- **Be Mindful.** Remain as objective as possible in assessing your feelings and thoughts. Keep your boundaries with limitations, while open to others and your opinions separate in order to hear the other side clearly.

- **Be Beautiful.** See the essence and beauty of everything that you touch, feel, or see. Seeing beauty gives us joy and love. The beauty of something is only real when you see deep within it.

- **Be True.** Regarding all your connections—both within your-self and with others—be authentic, rational, and specific, so as to communicate the problem clearly and identify any areas ripe for genuine compromise.

- **Be Your Best.** Only present your best and authentic self in all dealings and in all relationships. Know that your opinion counts and ensure that you pursue your goals with belief, trust, and honesty.

- **Be Passionate.** Allow only real feelings to have a place in your heart. Ensure that passion drives your ideals and goals; without compassion, caring, and concern for yourself and for others, nothing can be authentic.

Jung stated that true self-realization only occurs with integrity; integrity requires dealing with your unconscious complexes, such as the shadow, animus/anima, etc. The ability to keep yourself integrated involves conscious and observable behavior while being truthful and honest about all your characteristics. Jung and other great theorists on self-actualization and self-regulation, such as Abraham Maslow and Albert Bandura, make clear that your parts of self can work for you *or* against you—and that only you can manage yourself.

"Only I can change my life.
No one can do it for me."

—Carol Burnett

Maslow believed that self-actualization meant that certain needs of individuals, such as those involving physiology and safety, must precede those of belonging and self-esteem. Only then can self-actualization can occur. Bandura, on the other hand, believed that we learn through watching or imitating others and that managing our own growth requires self-regulation. Self-regulation involves being aware and keeping track of how we can be our best; managing our best-self involves balancing individual needs. We can also determine for ourselves the parts of self that help us become successful. As we learn how we learn, we can be more aware and focused. Educational psychology depends on teaching and learning strategies that facilitate this process; however, every individual is in charge of his or her own growth and development.

Personality Disorders

Male and female behavior can differ in any given situation. Some behavioral differences manifest in response to events, and some are innate personality disorders, many of which are more of a factor for men than they are for women. Research has shown that narcissism, for example, is a personality disorder that affects males more intensely than it does females. A narcissist puts his own interests and needs above those of his partner in a relationship. He feels the world rotates around him, and therefore has no boundaries. Without boundaries, power and energy are misaligned.

Jeffery Kluger, the author of *The Narcissist Next Door*, claims that many people can have narcissist tendencies, including your neighbors, family members, and coworkers that affect your relationships. The narcissists are able to manipulate people, until each person is lost in the world of the narcissist. Manipulation then becomes a way of life. Narcissistic leaders—mostly men—operate via manipulation; the effort produces the impression of power, but it is superficial and doesn't last. Women find more success as leaders when they eschew covert power strategies, such as manipulation, sex, or flattery.

In a book on narcissism entitled *Malignant Self-Love*, Dr. Sam Vaknin noted that all humans have emotions but that the narcissist tends to repress those emotions deeply; they play no conscious role in the narcissist's life. By repressing emotion the narcissist stashes his vulnerable true self in a deep cellar, outwardly presenting a false self and beginning to feel omnipotent and immune to the vicissitudes of the outside world. That's a recipe for disastrous leadership: An authentic leader must be open to emotion, and cognizant of other people's needs, allowing all to participate as a team without favoritism. Narcissistic tendencies can remove an otherwise great leader from the pulse and needs of those around him. It is imperative that leaders surround themselves with people who complement them. Leaders need to be aware.

Another alleged personality disorder is Attention Deficit Hyperactive Disorder (ADHD), also known as Attention Deficit Disorder (ADD). There is a great debate as to whether ADHD/ADD really exists or how it actually manifests itself in our behavior patterns, but, according to psychiatrist Daniel G. Amen, there are six major types of ADD, each presenting different emotional and mental challenges. People alleged to have ADD often have difficulty with decision-making, focus, and follow-through, and are generally restless, highly intelligent, out-of-the-box thinkers with attention problems. Counterintuitively, research indicates that many male CEOs are alleged to have ADD, a factor they must have been able to mitigate as they rose through the ranks. Once in a position of leadership, leaders alleged to have ADD or similar symptoms become a risk for the entire organization. Change throws these leaders off-balance; great leaders, by contrast, need to be able to adapt to change without losing focus on overall goals. ADD-burdened leaders have a tendency toward changing their minds, inconsistency, and failing to commit to the completion of critical tasks. Dr. Amen describes many CEOs as risk-takers who perform better when surrounded with people who keep them on track. He also believes diet and exercise play a big part in the ability to manage the alleged ADD.

Male/Female Behavior

Male and female behaviors are distinct in many ways, but some similarities exist. Both males and females have the characteristics to become great leaders. Generally, males tend to act authoritatively, taking over tasks deemed necessary; research shows, however, that success is far more common in the wake of consensus, collaboration, and participation of the whole. When met with challenges or conflicts, great leaders negotiate to get things accomplished; a leader must have a strong character to foster the belief of others and generate support. When leaders copy others or fail to convey belief in their own actions, then their authenticity and character can become suspect, and success is threatened. Authentic and truthful behavior encourages great leaders to be powerful.

Many male leaders who succeed despite their character traits, behavioral quirks, or personality disorders do so because they have a strong partner (often female) behind them to support their work. Many great female leaders have the support of their male partners who encourage them to succeed; however, the majority of great leaders are males supported by their partners. These relationships often follow the societal norm that sees men rewarded with credit and recognition. But the women behind these men often possess the necessary skills to be leaders themselves, if only they would step up and accept the role. One aspect of authentic leadership is recognizing a moment of opportunity when it presents itself.

- **We need to embrace our differences.** By understanding and accepting them, we can move forward to complete our tasks without gender bias. Males and female may see things differently but each can be taught to solve problems collaboratively with the other. We can accept our differences and work together.

- **We are all part of the world.** The world needs us as one entity, working for the good of the whole. The different parts of self can be unified in the view of the global perspective. The survival of the world depends on the extent to which we are able to work together. There is no other option. We know that we can solve problems together.

- **Male and female behaviors are often complementary.** Leaders excel at assessing the resources, talents, and practical tools available to accomplish goals. Male brains may be wired somewhat differently than female ones, but we can pool our thinking and feeling processes. Remember we each have male and female sides of ourselves.

There are successful male leaders, and successful female ones. The most successful, however, capitalize on male and female partnerships in which the differences are advantageous: men and women, working together, complementing each other rather than openly competing. This requires people who are conscious or mindful, with a strong sense of self and firm belief in others. Ego cannot be so powerful as to overtake the essence of others. Each of us has a male part of our self (animus) as well as a female part (anima); to maximize the likelihood of success—in a given task, in a leadership role, in life itself—these two aspects must be in sync. Our success as individuals, partners, or teams, depends on working together in this world of diversity and differences. Our male and females parts of self, if acknowledged, can work together. We must overcome conflict.

Brain Differences

Males and females exhibit differences in brain size as well as differences in ability within certain parts of the brain. Each individual is unique, however, and there may be female characteristics within a male brain and male characteristics within a female brain. Both the male and the female brain have several bridges connecting the left and right hemispheres. This process is complicated and unique for each individual. We use the term "bridge" in this context as an abstract theme. Any crossover can be considered a bridge, since the term is defined by Webster as *"a structure carrying a pathway over a depression or obstacle*, as well as *a means of connection or transition."* A bridge connects different ideas, people, and structures.

These bridges help us accomplish what we need most: the connection between males and females for the good of all, despite differences. All of us have to create these bridges, accepting all parts of self that are male or female, in all men and women. We can envision a bridge that can connect two opposing abstract ideas, a bridge that will finally end conflict or span great schisms that separate people from becoming the best they can be. We also need to construct bridges within ourselves and between others to accomplish difficult tasks or solve problems that afflict all of us. This bridge is also one that traverses the distance between what you desire for yourself and what you can (and will) accomplish. The bridge within the self includes the bridge between the body (your physical self) and the mind (your mental self), and ultimately the bridge to the spiritual self. Our world will succeed (and we will succeed within that world) when we have mastered the ability to construct all types of bridges.

Parts of the Brain

In the 2013 book *Super Brain*, Deepak Chopra and Rudolph Tanzi reduced the complex concept of the brain into a simplified notion comprising three main parts:

- **The Primate Brain** (lower part, or brain stem), which governs our instincts, our basic physiological (eating, sex, and survival) responses or needs, and primordial impulses, such as the fight-or-flight response;

- *The Limbic System* (middle of brain), which produces our emotional reactions, short-term memory, and the corpus callosum (or bridge), which governs activity between the brain's two hemispheres; and

- *The Frontal Cortex* (cognitive or front part of the brain), which governs decision-making, higher-order mental activities, impulsive guidance, and most of our thinking or choice-making functions.

The anterior cingulate cortex lies just under the frontal cortex in front of the corpus callosum, which participates in decision-making and governs the regulation of emotions, attention, and motivation (Amen, 2014). Amen views this as the gear-shifting mechanism, helping us to move on and to not hold grudges. This part of the brain also seems to govern understanding when we commit errors on a task; it helps to self-regulate and correct action or direction. Great leadership relies heavily on the anterior cingulate cortex, as do authenticity, responsibility, and great decision-making skills. All men and women have these parts in their brains; however, we are unique individuals, and no two brains are exactly alike. How they work remains a mystery.

Communication Differences

We do know that there are general differences between the male and female brains. Dr. Amen relates in his book *ADD*, for example, that there are different types of that disorder, and they typically afflict more men than women. Dr. Deborah Tannen, an important linguist of our era, has done intensive research in communication-specific gender differences. Admitting when mistakes occur, and reacting appropriately, is a vital trait for great leadership. Generally speaking, the middle part (corpus callosum) of the female brain appears to be larger than that of men; conversely, frontal cortices are larger in men. When men are focused, they do not generally like to be interrupted or given more than one task at a time. Women, on the other hand, generally excel at multitasking; however, they may lack focus. These generalizations *could* mean that female egos are less fragile and they can switch tasks more easily than those of their male counterparts— but the truth is we don't yet know for certain, as we still await results of ongoing research into these complementary differences.

A bridge, in its pure form, is merely a structure spanning opposing forces or providing passage over chasms and conflicts. (In simple architectural terms, for example, a bridge can be a horizontal piece—known as a lintel—connecting the tops of two columns.) In metaphorical terms, two parties connecting with each other over a bridge must have strong characters and authentic presentations since whatever is agreed upon must endure the passage of time. In this context, a bridge is "*a meeting of the minds.*" The brain is full of connecting impulses that fire to send messages from one part to another; thus the brain is a superstructure of multiple bridges.

If we overload a single bridge, it can collapse—causing confusion instead of conveying a message of information. Sometimes, leaders have to build many small bridges that connect to each other to get the full message across—a mesh of bridges, you might say. Bridges are everywhere. In telecommunications, for example, the Internet uses local area networks as small bridges to send messages across the global network. In discourse, we don't want to overload our audience, so we use smaller bridges of ideas—bite-sized concepts—to help us communicate our positions. Great leaders—great communicators—try to keep speeches and messages in digestible chunks, such as a short list of bullet-point ideas. Manageable bridges enable us to accomplish a great deal. As such, we will endeavor to build bridges between the understanding of males and females. Our goal is to balance our bridges to work together.

PART V

. . . .

PRINCIPLES FOR GREAT LEADERSHIP

"STAY CALM DURING TURBULENT TIMES. TO LEAD IN AN EVER-CHANGING WORLD, LEADERS MUST ADAPT AND STAY NIMBLE."

—Indra Nooyi

Some principles of great leadership are universal, and apply to both men and women; others depend on circumstance, the domain you're operating in, and what type of leader you hope to be. All leaders, for example, must be able to compromise, especially when engaged in partnerships. Historically, however, opportunities have been far more limited for female leaders. Given the privileges of the proverbial "*old boys' club*," male leaders have managed to ignore basic moral behavior and avoid issues that may have caused conflict. Women are inclined to seek out the truth and typically persevere until they do. As the old boys' club grows increasingly archaic, women have grown increasingly willing to speak up. Our society is finally encouraging them to do so. Multiple generations of women have now passed through the corporate world, and the mechanisms for discovering (and tolerating) fraud and other transgressions will never be the same.

Alan Greenspan, the former head of the Federal Reserve, reportedly once said: "*There is no need for regulation or stopping fraud since the markets will take care of themselves.*" During the 1990s, however, corporations began to disregard financial auditing procedures and compliance protocols. They became overly concerned with profits and started cutting corners, soon discovering they had the freedom to do what they wanted. The financial titans were arrogant, controlling, and dismissive of government interference. We all know the painful results of deregulation—and how we're still paying the price. In the latter half of the 20th century, we, as a society, struggled with gender differences, with male leaders fearful of losing their power and earning potential as females entered the executive sphere. In the early years of the 21st century, we've learned the truth that those fears were, to some extent, unfounded. Even as the Federal Reserve has seen its first female leader, the wage gap persists. Jill Abramson, for example, the first-ever female executive editor of *The New York Times*, was terminated in 2014 in part because she raised concerns that she was earning less than her (male) predecessor in the role. Women are beginning to speak up and we eventually hope this will make a difference.

Seven Principles of Leadership

Leaders need guidance and since their roles encompass a broad range of tasks and traits we have attempted to identify what we consider to be important. To provide the broadest possible foundation for discussion, we've selected the following principles of leadership that apply to both male and female leaders across many disciplines:

- *Success* is achieved when you rid yourself of the fear of failure. Be prepared to handle conflict by trusting yourself to take risks, having a clear vision, and adapting a plan. Belief in yourself supports your ability to keep your confidence high and behave nobly.

- *Initiative* is easily taken when you're honest and truthful, with clarity in your objectives. Authenticity and impeccable communication are required, while being mindful of boundaries. Your intentions have to be clear before taking any initiative.

- *Courage* isn't the absence of fear, but the ability to be brave in the face of it. Be brave in all actions; know yourself and how you can best face challenges or conflicts with resolve. Develop an independent spirit that reflects the essence of your leadership personality.

- *Passion* is necessary for your own motivation, and for your ability to inspire others. Enthusiasm is imperative for great decision-making. You have to be in a conscious state—self-aware—to act compassionately as a leader.

- *Cooperation* and compromise are necessary for the smooth resolution of conflict. Leaders develop a style that is noble in deed, prioritizing the good of all, and serving as a role model to encourage others to work together (and work well).

- *Intelligence* refers to wisdom of mind, body, and spirit, drawn from experience. That wisdom provides the ability to make timely and effective decisions and to resolve conflict. You must remain objective to solve problems mindfully and honestly.

- *Action* isn't merely about doing, but rather about treating all parties with respect. Your behavior must be tempered—mentally, emotionally, and spiritually. You must incorporate different opinions, but be decisive when the situation demands.

With these seven principles in mind, leaders exist on one of three stages of development:

1) *Novice*—The Beginning Stage: You are leading for the first time, assessing the environment and learning the terms of engagement. It takes time to learn a new environment; patience is required.

2) *Effective*—The Middle Stage: You are fully participating as a competent and successful leader. You are aware of your skills and talents and can incorporate your ideas when working with others.

3) *Inspirational*—The Latter Stage: You are an experienced leader and mentor, ready and willing to hand the baton to others you've trained to follow principles you've demonstrated.

The nuances of each of these stages may shift depending on the circumstances, the organization, and the industry. There may be many sub-stages depending on various disciplines. All leaders, however, follow a similar arc of progress, from novice, to effective, to inspirational.

"Optimism is the faith that leads to achievement.
Nothing can be done without hope and confidence."

—HELEN KELLER

Female Role Models

As we saw in Section One, many female role models have contributed a great deal to humanity. Florence Nightingale, for example, was a nurse who dedicated her life to helping others. She created hospitals for the poor and shared her nursing expertise with any who needed her care. In the 1500s, Saint Teresa of Ávila was a great advocate for the poor and for people in need, as was Mother Theresa, centuries later. The Bible talks about Queen Esther and other great queens who fought for their people. And then there was Queen Cleopatra of Egypt: a powerful, intelligent, an awesome Greek woman, descended from Alexander the Great. Cleopatra fought fiercely for her people, and may have been one of the most powerful rulers of all time. Plutarch wrote that *"Her actual beauty was far from being so remarkable that none could be compared with her, nor was it such that it would strike your fancy when you saw her first."* He also noted, however, that *"the influence of her presence, if you lingered near her, was irresistible; her attractive personality, joined with the charm of her conversation, and the individual touch that she gave to everything she said or did, were utterly bewitching."*

Saint Catherine and other saints such as, Saint Teresa of Avila were loved by their people and became patron saints equal in stature to their male counterparts. These saints were devoted to helping people and devoted to teaching about Christ to alleviate pain and suffering. There were other women also devoted to helping others. Helen Keller was blind and deaf and yet managed to write several books and travel the globe, giving hope to challenged people everywhere by sharing her experiences. Princess Diana helped children in need and worked to abolish the landmines that maimed and killed noncombatants. In addition to these real-life role models, many comic or fictional characters, such as Wonder Woman (whose golden lariat forced wrongdoers to speak the truth) and Katy Keene (a reporter who battled evil), have provided potential female leaders with inspiration. These fictional characters, like Batgirl, Supergirl, and all those who followed, still impact young children by offering powerful female role models.

During World War II, there were a group of female pilots called WASPs—Women Air Force Service Pilots—whose missions were so covert they were not recognized as part of the Air Force until 1977, even though many had sacrificed their lives to help our country win the war. Only then did they begin to receive veteran benefits. Finally, in 2009, they received the Congressional Gold Medal for valor in honor of their great deeds. There were undoubtedly many other groups of women over the years who sacrificed for the good of their country, many female spies and code breakers responsible for intelligence work that remains hidden to this day. The names of these women may be unknown to us, but they are no less heroic in stature. There have been many heroines and whistleblowers brave enough to speak up and tell the truth. We know of the female CIA analyst who dedicated five years to the search for Bin Laden's hideout in Pakistan, persevering even when all others thought the task impossible. In the 1990s, attorney Brooksley Born was warning Congress and the Federal Reserve about the inability to detect fraud, especially on derivatives. She was told not to continue her financial queries. Jacqueline Kennedy Onassis fought hard for the preservation of New York City's Grand Central Terminal as developers were threatening to tear it down. Earlier, as First Lady, she did admirable work in the renovation and redesign of the White House. Erin Brockovich uncovered fraud, fighting for compensation for the victims of cancer-causing pollution. The movies *Norma Rae* and *Silkwood* depicted the plight of women in factories. Recently Christine Driscoll-O'Neill, who wrote *Searching for Justice: Finding Hope* (2013), blew the whistle on kickbacks to doctors from pharmaceutical firms. She spent many years searching for the truth since the expensive drugs were not working for the AIDS patients. She had the courage to speak the truth and perseverse to bring attention to injustice.

Woman and Justice

Another great recent female leader, Elizabeth Warren, is the senior United States Senator from Massachusetts. Warren wrote *A Fighting Chance*, recalling her life and her stand for the plight of the middle class, having spent 10 years trying to get the government to provide better bankruptcy laws for the common man. We can glean that her attributes and traits are laudable for great leadership in this country. We encourage more women like Elizabeth Warren to speak out about the simple truth and what we need in our country now.

We also hope Hillary Clinton continues pursuing roles to make the most of her great leadership skills; she may be the most experienced woman in our modern political system. Other potential female leaders like Olympia Snowe, is a retired republican senator (2013) from Maine. Olympia was named one of America's 10 Best Senators in 2006 by *Time* magazine. She was chairman of the committee focusing on small business concerns.We encourage more women to speak out and take on great leadership roles. We believe that the time is now and our culture is ready.

It is self-evident that women are capable of great leadership; however, they can also sabotage each other. During the 1970s-era battle over the Equal Rights Amendment, which never passed, women essentially took polarized positions without reaching any consensus or common ground, effectively undermining their collective strength as they became divided. Unresolved issues regarding women and power extended to domestic life, as well. Some women wanted to be housewives and wield their power covertly. Some, whose high-profile husbands had affairs, had to decide whether to *"stand by my man,"* balancing their own dignity against the covert power of a political marriage. And some high-profile women continue to target other powerful women; when Sarah Palin was a candidate for vice president, for example, Katie Couric attacked her (and Tina Fey parodied her) with a vengeance. Regardless of political validity, the attacks were embarrassing, spotlighting the negative qualities often ascribed to women. This kind of competition is lethal. We have not witnessed this type of behavior where men ridicule other men to benefit their career to this relentless degree. It is much simpler to be overt and develop one's own power. Even acknowledging the value of a successful partnership, there is nothing like independence, knowing you can accomplish whatever you put your mind to.

Leadership and Essentialism

There is a great debate about the personality of human beings: How much of an individual's persona depends on nature (innate characteristics), and how much on nurture (outside influences) and the environment in which a person grows up. Freud believed that our personalities are established by age 5; several of his students, however—such as Erik Erikson and Carl Jung—stated that there were great influences from the environment. We don't believe in the strict concept of *essentialism;* in our view the truth involves a combination of both innate and the environment. *Essentialism* holds that there are innate and essential differences between males and females and that we are born with certain traits— traits, for example, that preclude women from excelling in math and science. Yes there are innate traits but these traits can be changed. Essentialism belittles women and propagates bias on women being limited.

Recent brain studies have led many social biologists who believe in essentialism to claim that there are some genetic differences and that our male/female gender identity is innate. We disagree: Yes, there are differences between men and women, but we often see male traits in females, and vice versa, so blanket gender-specific assertions have too many exceptions to be valuable. For centuries, our society and culture successfully deterred females from pursuing male-dominated disciplines such as science and math. Only recently have women begun to see opportunities in these areas, as their strength in accepting their power has grown.

The argument that males and females are inherently different has been argued for eons—at least as far back as Aristotle, who believed that females were (and should be) subordinate to males; he believed that a male and female of the same species were essentially different. Plato had more of an egalitarian viewpoint. According to Raewyn Connell, an Australian sociologist and researcher, *biological essentialism* itself evolved as an explanation of male dominance that emphasized differences in size and in muscular strength. The theory states that males supposedly had hormone-based "*aggressive advantages*" and fixed ways of learning. This notion insults both genders, since there are many different ways of learning. Connell also wrote that "*the idea that gender relations are biologically fixed is shown up as nonsense in the light of the ethnographic and historical evidence of cultural diversity and change.*" We need to build a genuine scientific understanding of gender relations, an undertaking that's only just begun. We believe that our humanity and creativity reflect the highest form of self, with gender or sex at the base. Creativity has no sex.

Intelligence has no sex. Individuals are unique. In this modern age we should be well beyond gender boundaries and limitations.

It is easy to use *"essentialism"* to control women, to diminish their power and individuality. But all humans have the same potential to succeed and the same right to be judged based on their respective talents and skills. Just as men are not all alike, neither are women. Some have scientific proclivities; some do not. Society, however, has strongly suggested that women are ill-suited to science and logic, stifling their attempts to make the most of any skills or interest they might have. Women in general have a desire to seek out truth—an attribute shared by many great scientists and philosophers. We know that many great scientists have been women, or women working with men. Today, we see an increasing number of women displaying diverse skills across all disciplines, to the benefit of all: Women and men can enhance each other and support each other's successes.

Gender Integration

Earlier generations had to be shown the truth of society's racial bias; now we need to be aware of its gender bias. It is time for all to wake up and see that society has refused to acknowledge the full scope of female capabilities. We can integrate the workplace with the full capacity of both men and women. Bias and prejudice are obstacles to a progressive society that relies on knowledge, acceptance, and understanding. Unleashing the true power of both sexes will surely advance our society and the globe. The truth is that both sexes need to work together to reach our potential. U.S. Senator Elizabeth Warren, for example, often speaks of the plight of the middle class and the need for our children to be protected by the government. Her voice supersedes gender. Both men and women listen to her; when she speaks, we do not hear "a woman's voice," but rather that of an intelligent, logical, and coherent person who is concerned for the future of our country and the well being of all its citizens. We are all human, and our gender is merely a physical side of self with minimal importance. All human beings, men and women, should have equal opportunity.

We can integrate males and females without putting emphasis on gender. Gender bias is similar to racism; both are based on superficial judgments that overemphasize the importance of appearance. We ignore the true value of a person when we look only at what's on the surface—gender, color, or both. True power resides beneath the surface; we cannot allow our judgments to hinder female performance. For example, Jill Abramson was fired as executive editor of *The New York Times* after she discovered she was earning less than her male predecessor had been, and sought equal pay. Abramson was considered "pushy" when she confronted her superiors—an adjective rarely used to describe male leaders. She was chastised for several issues, including "arbitrary decision-making and a failure to consult with colleagues." Many male leaders make arbitrary decisions and do not consult with their colleagues. While we may not know the full story, we do know that she was a woman who asked for equal pay. We as a nation need to put equal-pay issues to rest. Our country can make this happen. We have great female leaders. We are ready.

PART VI

ATTRIBUTES FOR
BUILDING BRIDGES

"WE NEVER KNOW HOW HIGH WE ARE

TILL WE ARE ASKED TO RISE

AND THEN IF WE ARE TRUE TO PLAN

OUR STATURES TOUCH THE SKIES."

—Emily Dickinson

The greatest leaders possess qualities that reinforce and extend the best aspects of their personas. The authentic self is strong—strong enough to lead—and soulful or spirited in belief, which inspires others and encourages them to be their best. According to Plato, the ancient Greek philosopher, *psyche* is the Greek word for *soul*—the essence of a person or how one behaves authentically. Other connotations for soul involve acting morally or depicting the essential nature of a person including their true sense of identification. Some people confuse *spirit* and *soul*, such as an independent spirit or a soulful person. In this context, we tend to agree with the ancient Greeks and assume that *spirit* comes from the Greek word for *breath* or *living*, while the soul is the essence that powers the creation of an event or other artistic endeavors. The soul has no gender.

According to Pythagoras in the 6th century BC, a Greek philosopher and mathematician, gender was not an issue. He believed that the souls of males and females were equal since he allowed females in his academies to study along with his famous male students. Connections between great leaders encourage strong, soulful individuals to inspire others with their spirit. Neither the soul nor the spirit has a gender. Males and females are equal in the realm of the spiritual self. The soulful leader is moral, and mindful that her noble behavior is an example to others and benefits the community or the world. After the 4th century BC, the status of women changed.

Integrated Leaders

Great leaders possess their own sense of power. They have enormous energy that they share with others, adhering to clear boundaries that allow them to lead with conviction and to model behavior for others to follow. Authentic leaders are present and in the moment so they can connect with others and convey their messages; they are in touch with their souls and aware of their strengths. Integrated people have purpose; they are in touch with their *"calling."* The following 5 *Cs* are emblematic of great, integrated leaders:

- *Confidence*—Feelings of self-worth (high self-esteem) are needed to convert a leader's authentic intent into actions fortified by conviction. Personal power depends on self-esteem,

self-concept, and boundaries; confidence ensures power is
not lost or weakened during conflicts.

- **Conscientiousness**—Mindfulness (being present and aware)
  is needed when working with others, allowing leaders to be
  knowledgeable and responsible for all their actions. This also
  implies being in the present moment, alert, and not overly
  dwelling on past situations or problems.

- **Consistency**—Truth and honesty must be substantial to be
  recognized. Changing your mind for no apparent reason
  undermines your position as a great leader. A leader cannot
  waffle or waver; adaptation, on the other hand, is often necessary, as circumstances dictate.

- **Compassion**—Caring about and listening to the needs of the
  populace are required for great leadership. Superficial feelings
  are fleeting and obstruct leadership. Because leaders inspire
  by projecting strength, belief, and power of conviction, an
  authentic leader must be genuine in his or her feelings when
  connecting to others.

- **Communication**—Communication is an obvious prerequisite
  to great leadership but projecting ideas *clearly* requires that
  messages be truthful, concise, and pertinent. Leaders must
  not overwhelm their audience; it's the leader's responsibility
  to deliver information in palatable pieces that people
  can connect to and remember.

A truly confident leader is consistent and clearly conveys her
vision to the majority, taking proper measure of her thoughts and

ideas. She leads with compassion and spirit, maintaining focus on priority goals. Her true sentiment is strong and authentic and she projects a self that is never hostile. People who lack true confidence will put others down through sarcastic humor or by denigrating others' behavior. An integrated soul generates concern, compassion, and sympathy for others.

Leadership Activities

Your purpose in life is to pursue your personal spiritual journey, and that journey requires you to continually build bridges that connect you to our goals. Great leaders know that there are many types of bridges, including the bridge between the parts of self, and the bridges we create to connect to others. You have to build a bridge to your own soul so that you can be creative, an authentic leader, and who you truly are. The soul, in turn, is the bridge between our mind and brain. Our mind contains abstract thoughts and feelings, while our brain provides the physical processing of our concrete thoughts. Communication occurs via our actions and behavior. After building internal bridges we build external ones to connect with people in order to create common ground or a meeting of minds.

Authentic leaders construct authentic bridges. The construction of these bridges is hardly the end of your spiritual or soulful journey, which is an ongoing process requiring your constant care and attention. Authentic leaders are always engaged in a series of leadership activities, which can embody qualities ranging from the obvious to the subtle. They include the following:

- Act with optimism.
- Avoid negative energy and criticism.
- Share knowledge.
- Maintain a clear vision of goals.
- Foster creativity and imagination.
- Communicate your ideals, goals, and next steps.
- Manage projects effectively.
- Believe in yourself and others.
- Value emotional intelligence and compassion.
- Learn the value of content and context.
- Pursue noble actions with realistic goals and ideals.
- Be consistent in leadership style, yet adjust or adapt when necessary.
- Delegate fairly, assigning tasks appropriately.
- Compromise if required, without sacrificing yourself.
- Lead bravely, teaching followers to overcome fear.
- Acknowledge others, and respect them.
- Encourage others, and engage with them.
- Listen to others, and collaborate with them.
- Motivate others, and guide them.
- Inspire others, and trust them.
- Teach trust within the team.

The personalities of great leaders are best reflected by their behavior when resolving problems. These leaders possess various problem-solving skills, perhaps the most critical of which is the ability to assess and respect clear boundaries. This enables leaders to listen and be coherent when solving problems. As role models, great leaders have to manage their own behavior. We lose respect for them if they become too emotional. Their selfish needs undermine potential resolutions—to global problems as well as simple tasks. If they do not have or respect spiritual boundaries, leaders become narcissists and miss the essence of truth. Great leaders cannot afford to take things personally (via projections, assumptions, or misunderstandings). They can't allow anything to hinder their ability to communicate effectively. Need proof? Imagine a room full of self-centered or extroverted individuals trying to solve a problem: all talking at once, failing to resolve anything. They are only concerned with winning and competing with each other. We are experiencing this within the current political leadership of our country.

Leaders and Adaptability

History is our great teacher. Change is ever-present and strong leaders must adapt. By being honest, open, and creative, they meet all sorts of challenges and overcome them with vision and perseverance. Examples of authentic leadership abound: personalities, actions, and beliefs that together reveal a clear picture of character, philosophy, and accomplishments. The best of our current and past leaders should be our role models: influential in their own time, and exemplars for future leaders. We only need to be open to learn from the great deeds and mistakes of others.

- Many male leaders, in various fields, had to adapt to constant change: politics and war (Alexander the Great, Winston Churchill, Abraham Lincoln, Benjamin Franklin); the confluence of science, technology, business, and innovation (Thomas Edison, Nikola Tesla, Bill Gates, Steve Jobs); and shifts in society and philosophy (Leo Tolstoy, Henry James). We can learn from their conflicts and accomplishments.

- Many female leaders also had to muster courage in the face of challenges: political leaders in times of war or unrest (Margaret Thatcher, Aung San Suu Kyi); authors or artists cataloguing societal shifts (Jane Austen, Edith Wharton, Coco Chanel, Sheryl Sandberg); and innovators battling resistance (Marie Curie, Amelia Earhart, Grace Hopper). These leaders had to fight many battles to become who they are. Each discipline has its heroines.

- Some female leaders ruled entire nations; they deserve special recognition, for their outsize position in history: Queen Elizabeth I and Queen Victoria of England; Catherine the Great of Russia; Cleopatra, Hatshepsut, and Nefertiti—three of the greatest female rulers of Egypt; Catherine de Medici of France; Queen Isabella of Spain; Mary, Queen of Scots (Mary I of Scotland); Tzu-Hsi, the "dowager empress" of China from 1835 to 1908; and Lili'uokalani, the last

monarch (and only queen regnant) of Hawaii (1838-1917).
There were also many queens and female warriors from
Africa and the ancient world.

Many leaders' stories were actually tales of successful partnerships
or collaborations, some of which thrived despite adversity: in politics
(Queen Victoria and Albert; Franklin and Eleanor Roosevelt; John F.
Kennedy and his brother Robert F. Kennedy; Bill and Hillary Clinton);
philosophy, psychology, and science (Hypatia and her father; Plato
and his teacher Socrates; Albert Einstein and wife Mileva; Francis
Crick and James Watson; Erik Erikson and wife Joan); the arts (Helen
Keller and Anne Sullivan; Fred Astaire and Ginger Rogers; Lucille Ball
and her husband Desi Arnaz); and business (Gianni Versace and his
sister Donatella; Dr. Roy and Diana Vagelos; Bill and Melinda Gates).

The stories of these various leaders and partnerships are the ones
that changed our lives, thanks to their passion, focus, diligence,
bravery, integrity, belief, drive, ethics (moral philosophy), and innovation. Their stories have been instructive, but it's incumbent upon
us to actively apply these lessons to our own projects. We need role
models to guide future leaders, especially young girls seeking their
place in the world. In sum, great leaders need to:

- Be True;
- Be Brave;
- Be Just;
- Be Honest; and
- Be Smart.

Leaders need to be able to depend on those that are on their teams and their job is keep the communication and connection continuous for loyalty, competency, and acceptance since everyone must feel that they are all on the same page. Great leaders surround themselves with people they trust and with their consistent and just behavior their followers will always be there to support their visions and goals.

Cause and Effect for Leaders

Society has trained men to believe that women think in a cursory way, but the opposite is true. The heightened sensitivity that women typically possess may only appear to varying degrees, but consistently more so than in men. Sensitivity breeds a degree of insight valuable in authentic decision-making. Fortunately, an ever-expanding number of men relish female counsel and honor its source by elevating women to the places they deserve. Even these men, however, are often merely seeking a "female perspective"; we should instead promote greater depth from all women. We must remember that "we reap what we sow."

Our greatest dilemma is that American-led global culture thrives on competition and a flawed view of the economy. Both genders are taught that individual wins are more important than collaborative victories. For this reason, the female persona is dismissed as insignificant. Contrary to the Darwinian notion of "survival of the fittest," research in quantum physics and biology has proven that we are all wired for community, caring, and love. It is now well established that unified consciousness and universal connectivity reign overall. We must identify faulty premises that burden us, and unshackle ourselves from previously accepted ideas. Since we all truly want harmony, togetherness, support, and security, it is time that we authentically invite the female voice into critical discussion.

Sharing Power

To date, women's power has been restricted, or at least discouraged, or at the very least marginalized. It is time for us to abolish these disgraces. Until the female voice is heard, and authentically given the freedom to participate in decisions, humanity is working at half speed. How do we get there? We begin now and continue our quest. We know that both males and female have much to offer each other and sharing the power is a relief for both genders.

First, we have to reassure men that their genuine desires to follow their own paths are cherished. Once they are put at ease, they are more likely to want the same for those they love. Exaggerating one's own masculinity—and the related insecurities—can be exhausting for a man. If he were able to allow his heart to govern his primitive thoughts, his protective instincts would allow for the possibility (and perhaps see the potential rewards) of being a supportive friend. Fear must not win. Many men, especially in the nineties, feared that women would take their place and their identity would be lost. Some men set out to embarrass women, to disrespect them, and to humiliate them so that they only men would look good and be the winners. Men cannot look at sharing power as a competition, but as teamwork that must share knowledge to survive. We must learn to respect each other.

The Hormonal Reality

Hormones affect both men and women. For example, the male hormone testosterone is allegedly the aggressive hormone that allows males to show their power and strength; estrogen is the female hormone that gives women their feminine characteristics. The reality, however, is that both women and men produce testosterone *and* estrogen, in various degrees. Women can be as aggressive as males; however, our society still expects women to be subordinate rather than "pushy" or "bossy." As we progress, we hope to see the elimination of such biased, gender-centric notions of behavior from our judgments and expectations. We should begin to accept each other as individuals, embracing behaviors that are the result of each person's unique blend of genetics, experience, background, and unique environment, a combination of factors that make us able to give each other the gift of ourselves.

Our sex hormones also govern our attraction to one another, but they do not produce the emotional maturity that is needed for a supportive partnership. All too often, the woman must spearhead the construction of a bridge to support tenderness and transparency. In part, this requires first bridging the animus/anima within, reaching a plateau of excellence that lays the groundwork for the harmonious and peaceful world to which we all aspire. Mutual respect, uncalculated support, and abundant kindness are the resulting benefits of balance, leading in turn to secure women, men, families, and humanity. We will only achieve this universal security by freeing women from their own—as well as societal—shackles. Central to this change is the ability to listen to one another without relying on preconceived notions. Both males and females have to deal with their hormonal realities, acknowledging the limited role they play in the formation of our authentic selves rather than allowing them to define us.

Liberation of the Female Spirit

"Women, like men, should try to do the impossible.
And when they fail, their failure should
be a challenge to others."

—AMELIA EARHART

We should prioritize *the authentic liberation of the female spirit*. This spirit is our mother, protector, and perpetuator. Women have a spiritual knowledge situated deep within their souls and honed by the application of selfless fact. Unity of soul and heart makes available a limitless pool of potential, and enables females to speak fearlessly. (Men, too, will benefit from the shift in direction.) There have been historical moments that spotlighted this goal; sadly, gender-based fear has always undermined any potential for progress. Even the most advanced cultures—those that have approached some semblance of female freedom—have eventually crumbled. So it's fair to ask: Is this an impossible goal? And, if not, how might today's society fare any better? It's essential to have faith in the idea that many things once believed impossible have actually come to pass. This, too, can be achieved, embraced, and replicated. Like all other progressive endeavors, the process begins with people willing to reinvent the wheel. Creativity is the result of putting the pieces back together in a different way.

Imagine if we taught each little girl to see her heart as her greatest asset, primed for enrichment through knowledge. Imagine young boys taught from an early age to perceive females as their colleagues and equals. This vision can only be realized through the advancement of potent examples: women who have broken the mold of old paradigms and established new standards. By consistently falling back into tired roles, we prevent the acceleration and acceptance of female leadership. Expecting support—or, worse, waiting for some—before pursuing a new reality is just folly. Become the dream and create the new reality through force of will and the certainty that the goal is just.

Problem Solving for Leaders

Becoming a great leader involves the ability to make decisions effectively and to solve problems analytically, through either inductive or deductive reasoning.

- The decision-making process involves identifying the relevant information and then applying the best means of making the most intelligent choice.
- Inductive reasoning involves first looking at details before tracing back to general information on the decision-making topic.
- Deductive reasoning involves looking at the general information first and then analyzing it to get to the detail.
- Analysis breaks down the gathered information into smaller concepts that can be understood easily. Synthesis or creative

thinking puts together these pieces of information into an original concept that can aid in decision-making. The more familiar you are with the material under discussion, the more easily you can make the decision.

One business dictionary describes decision-making as *"the thought process of selecting a logical choice from the available options: When trying to make a good decision, a person must weigh the positives and the negatives of each option and consider all the alternatives; for effective decision-making, a person must be able to forecast the outcome of each option as well, and based on all these items, determine which option is the best for that particular situation."* As leaders, we are constantly barraged with information that may or may not be pertinent. Our job is to discern and discard what is not relevant. Once we have an adequate amount of pertinent information, then we can resume the process of making intelligent and appropriate decisions. Decision-making implies elimination until the best course of action reveals itself.

A decision is, at its core, a project. Running businesses throughout our careers, we have had extensive experience with project management: planning, organizing, motivating, and controlling procedures to achieve specific goals. Time management is also an essential part of this process.

PART VII

••

INTERVIEWS ON LEADERSHIP

"Now if you or any other really intelligent person were arranging the fairness and justices between man and woman, you give the man a one-fiftieth interest of one women, and the woman a harem."

—Mark Twain

Mark Twain was a great American lecturer, author and openly discussed the inequality of race and gender. We respect his views, humor, and honesty. He traveled the world sharing his experiences and humor to sold-out audiences. We wanted male leaders to participate in our survey and we were fortunate to have this happen. We also value female perspectives. Dr. Maria Montessori revolutionized the education system during a time when children with learning disabilities became outcasts and her system of teaching using the five senses was adapted by the world. We value male/female perspectives and thus our interviews were born.

"Establishing lasting peace is the work of education;
all politics can do is keep us out of war."

–MARIA MONTESSORI

We interviewed men and women great leaders who have developed the attributes, personalities, and vision for success. Seven questions gave some structure to the interviews; however, we allowed the interviewees the freedom to discuss what they felt was important.

ABOUT THE INTERVIEWEES

DR. KARL K. STEVENS

Dr. Karl K. Stevens has over 50 years of professional engineering and university teaching experience. He spent more than 30 of those years at Florida Atlantic University (FAU), in Boca Raton, Fla., culminating in a decade spent as dean of FAU's College of Engineering and Computer Science. Dr. Stevens came to FAU after more than a decade on the engineering faculty of the Ohio State University. He also held positions at the Sandia Corp. in Albuquerque, N.M., Bell Telephone Laboratories, and the U.S. Army Ballistic Research Laboratory.

After becoming dean of FAU's College of Engineering and Computer Science in 2001, Dr. Stevens had management responsibility for a program with 2,200 students, 160 faculty and staff, annual externally funded research expenditures in excess of $12 million, and an annual budget of some $25 million. Dr. Stevens previously served as associate dean for academic affairs (1993–2001), chair of the Department of Mechanical Engineering (1991–1993) and chair of Ocean Engineering (1981–1983). He was professor of Ocean Engineering from 1978 to 1983 and of Mechanical Engineering from 1983 to 2011. His greatest accomplishment at FAU, however, is the creation and management of the new "green" engineering building, working with a team he put together of staff members, colleagues, and coworkers.

Dr. Stevens is the recipient of the FAU Presidential Leadership Award and 12 major awards for excellence in teaching and research. Kansas State University named him a Charter Member of its Engineering Hall of Fame in 1989. *The South Florida Business Journal* named him its *"Heavy Hitter"* for Administration in 2006. He continues to receive accolades for his work and is writing books about his life and wonderful canine companions. He is known for his eccentric sense of humor and his colleagues were very sad to see him retire since he kept the department exciting in an otherwise pedantic atmosphere. His keen interest in new projects keep him going strong.

DR. SUSANNE LAPP

Dr. Susanne I. Lapp is an associate professor of education at Florida Atlantic University (FAU). She received her doctorate in Curriculum and Instruction from the University of Cincinnati with a focus on English for Speakers of Other Languages (ESOL) and technology. Her master's degree is on second-language literacy with emergent readers. A former ESOL instructor of graduate students, she later served as an assistant professor at the University of Texas–Pan American, specializing in literacy education. In addition to teaching courses in FAU's undergraduate and graduate teacher-education programs, she has also served as the founding interim chair of FAU's Curriculum, Culture, and Educational Inquiry department and as division chair and professor of education at Seton Hill University in Greensburg, Pa. Her administrative expertise contributes to her well-organized courses.

Susanne Lapp is an excellent professor and is noted for her ability to simplify complex ideas that can be easily understood by her students. Her personality is affable, enthusiastic, and always there to help other colleagues and her students. Lapp is highly regarded, respected, and well-liked by all her students and other professors; she is known as a team player. She travels extensively to Europe and brings forth a wealth of knowledge of not only her content area but also of the world. Her student evaluations are of the highest caliber.

Lapp has coauthored several books (such as, *Literacy, Language, and Culture: Methods and Strategies for Mainstream Teachers with Diverse Learners;* also, *Building a Literacy Community: Strategies for Authentic Assessment; and Exploring Language Arts through Children's & Adolescent Literature*), and has made over 60 national and international presentations and contributed to publications that concentrate on educational technology and language acquisition. Susanne is well-known in her field as an accomplished authority on literacy and learning secondary languages. Her great accomplishments speak for themselves.

DR. BRIAN R. CLEMENT

Dr. Brian Clement is the director of the renowned Hippocrates Health Institute (HHI), the world's foremost complementary residential health center, where he and his team have developed a state-of-the-art program for health maintenance and recovery. HHI has pioneered a life-changing program, establishing training in active aging and disease prevention that has been shown to raise health and happiness levels. HHI's philosophy is founded on the belief that a plant-based, living, enzyme-rich diet, complemented by exercise, positive thinking, and non-invasive therapies, is integral to optimum health. As stated nearly 2,500 years ago by Hippocrates, the father of modern medicine: *"Let food be thy medicine and medicine be thy food."* Dr. Clements is an engaging teacher on this topic.

A natural lecturer and performer, Clement worked his way through college as a musician. He became a vegetarian, losing a substantial amount of weight, enhancing his overall health. Later, he became a complete vegan. He was determined to help others find what he had found and has dedicated his life to this pursuit. His exuberant personality is contagious and his audiences enjoy his lectures while they are learning about a healthy life-style.

On behalf of HHI, Clement went to Europe and educated Europeans about the raw-food movement. In 1978 he spent a year in Denmark, as director of the Humlegaarden Institute, founded by Danish raw-food pioneer Dr. Kristine Nolfi in the early 1940s. In 1980 he returned to the United States and became director of HHI, which he and his wife, Dr. Anna Maria Clement, moved to Florida in 1987. The Institute now provides seminars, lectures, and educational programs. Traveling to more than 40 countries, Clement has helped thousands improve their lives and take control of their health through the use of natural foods. He has written numerous books examining health, spirituality, and natural healing. One of his bestselling books is *Living Foods for Optimum Health*, and with his wife Dr. Anna Maria Clement he co-authored *7 Keys to Lifelong Sexual Vitality*. He also recently co-authored, with Dr. Katherine Powell, *Belief: Integrity in Relationships*. He continues to write books that are on the cutting edge.

LAVINIA LEE MEARS, Esq.

Lavinia Lee Mears is an attorney, business consultant, and copywriter with more than 20 years of professional experience. As a business consultant, Mears has advised organizations in the areas of marketing, operational efficiency, and strategic planning. She has developed employee-solution-based cost-saving programs and advised senior management on effectively handling organizational change during restructuring and downsizing. Mears's legal practice primarily focuses on the issues of employment and commercial, consumer, and criminal law. She advises organizations on how to avoid employee litigation and has been retained to oversee several corporate investigations. Mears also is a court-appointed mediator who has helped parties to navigate alternative dispute-resolution procedures. She is well-known her field and is in demand for her services.

Lavinia has many talents including: Speaking before audiences, planning marketing strategies, and has also edited work of other colleagues and students. Her personality is immediately infectious and has garnered great success from her ability to communicate with agility and preciseness. Her ability to assess situations quickly and to advise others in finding adequate solutions is an asset to whatever jobs she accepts. You can only smile when with her.

A seasoned trial attorney, Mears served as a County Assistant Prosecutor for the State of New Jersey before entering corporate practice. As an attorney for a major telecommunications corporation, Lavinia negotiated numerous hundred-million-dollar contracts for high-end technology products and services. She has received several professional awards, and was named to New Jersey Biz Magazine's "40 Under 40" list (as one of the state's top 40 most influential young business leaders) and to the New Jersey Association of Women Business Owners' "NJAWBO 30" (recognizing the state's 30 most successful female business owners). Her enthusiasm for life and delving into new adventures keep her motivated and always moving.

1. What axiom do you feel is the secret to your success, the most important mantra in keeping your leadership unique?

Dr. Karl K. Stevens: *I believe you have to have a clear and an unequivocal vision of what is to be accomplished. People have to work together to get the work done. For example, I developed a highly effective Engineering Executive Advisory Council comprising some 25 executive-level leaders from business and industry. I worked with them to create and fund a unique Innovation Leadership Honors Program for undergraduates and collaborated on numerous other key program, research, and development issues. Everyone had a different background and each had their own ideas; however, our priority was to keep our focus and vision intact and to contribute to our main cause. Working with people of different backgrounds is very educational; each person can learn from the others. It is important when working with others to become a participatory leader and not be dogmatic in your leadership style. Everyone has something to contribute, so my mantra is to be patient and listen to what they need and what they have to say.*

Dr. Susanne Lapp: *That's a very interesting question. My leadership experience has generally consisted of serving in the capacity of an interim chair of a newly created department, and my other major administrative role was that of as a division chair of an entire academic discipline*

(Education). As a division chair, I was the supervisor and administrator over the following programs of study: educational leadership; exceptional-student education; and early childhood, elementary, and secondary education. I had to lead several accreditation proceedings while adjusting to an entirely new position within an entirely new set of academic expectations (a private, Catholic, liberal arts college). Frequently, I found myself acting as my own academic and professional mentor and as a result, often turned to my earliest forms of guidance: biblical scripture. Several verses from the Bible seem to stand out as my guiding "mantras"—or, shall I say, spiritual life preservers—which I turned to, especially when dealing with the challenging situations that are constantly present in the life of a department/division chair. The first verse comes from the book of Romans (Romans 8:31) in the New Testament, which states, "If God is for us, who can be against us?" Another very uplifting verse that I frequently reflected on is Psalm 118:6 "The Lord is with me. I will not be afraid. What can mere mortals do to me?"

Dr. Brian R. Clement: *First, I have no aspiration to be a unique leader but more so an effective one. Leading by example, in my mind, is the only effective method. If you are not willing to do something yourself, it is disingenuous to expect your coworkers to do so effectively. The secrets to my success are perseverance, relentlessness, and love of life.*

Following your heart is the only effective approach to find what you love—but society often discourages us from doing so, our culture and parental upbringing misguidedly urging us to follow money rather than purpose. When you do find what you love, and you dedicate yourself to your work's integrity, an organic process naturally occurs, allowing you to excel. People's passion is contagious—a positive pathogen that is effortlessly passed on to the conscious people around you. Fulfilled, focused, and forthright people are rare in our homogenized, valueless society, a scarcity that merely serves to underscore the dire need for this type of committed leadership. Working side by side with people who are capable—and empowering them to do the best that they can with their own skills—is far more effective than attempting to mold unwilling people into uncomfortable and untenable positions. Open dialogue, mutual respect, and, most important, professional acknowledgement should be laced in all coworker relationships.

If your heart is first with devotion and dedication your mind and body will follow. What you do as a leader is then authentic and true to your vision and goals.

Lavinia Lee Mears, Esq.: *Relationships are everything. People follow and do business with people they know, like, and trust. That is the common thread behind my successes, both professionally and personally. Having good relationships is not something that I plan. I don't consciously set out to ensure I have good relationships with people as a means to an end. I don't say, "I'm going to get in good with Jane Doe so that I can accomplish a specific goal." For the most part, it happens naturally. Success is often an inadvertent*

*by-product of a positive (and previously fostered) relation-
ship. Like most people, whatever I am trying to accomplish,
whether it is personal or professional, almost always requires
the cooperation and buy-in of at least one other person.
Clients must choose to hire you for your business to prosper.
Judges and juries must be persuaded to rule in your client's
favor to win. Employees have to give you their best work for
your company to shine.*

*My mentor, the late, great Walter Lucas, drilled into my
head how success in the legal profession relied on cultivat-
ing relationships. Most important, he stressed how critical it
was to foster positive relationships with "adversaries"—the
attorneys on the other side of the case. He gave me a T-shirt
for my law school graduation which read,* "A good lawyer
knows the law. A great lawyer knows the judge." *It was
Walter's gentle way of cautioning me not to let my fiercely
competitive spirit stand in the way of my success. He often
said,* "Clients will come and go. The attorneys you see in
court every day are the ones that you have to deal with
for the rest of your life." *How true Walter's advice would
prove to be. Eventually, I began going to Bar Association
functions—events that usually took place at night and left
me feeling out of place as one of the very few women in
attendance.* "So this is what 'the old boys' club' looks like,"
*I would think to myself. I struggled through my discomfort
and eventually I began meeting lawyers and judges.*

2. What accomplishments are you most proud to have been part of, and how did you achieve these successes?

Dr. Karl K. Stevens: *I'll mention just one: the funding, planning, construction, and occupancy of a 97,000-square-foot building that achieved LEED certification at the Platinum Level—a certification never before achieved in the southeast United States. It was pooh-poohed by some experts who said it couldn't be done in Florida because of the high humidity. Academic buildings tend to be guarded jealously by their occupants; I wanted a building that was welcoming to all. Focus typically is on faculty offices and labs; I wanted a building that also provided great facilities for students. Several years prior, I had identified additional space as a top need for our college. Yet every year we were slipping lower on the university's list of priorities for facilities funding. I knew I needed a "hook."*

Environmental—or "green"—issues were coming to the forefront at that time and I thought a move in this direction might give us some added traction. I discussed the idea with a staff member, who had broad experience in business and industry. She agreed, and we were off and running. When all was said and done, we ended up with a modern, LEED-certified building that provided great facilities for faculty and students.

Several elements, many of which we did not foresee up front, were key to our ultimate success: (1) The University architect was supportive of the idea of "going green;" (2) Our new president liked the idea of his university being "first" in something; (3) We included a world-class student center in the design; and, (4) We welcomed all to utilize whatever food service we might have. It's also important to remember that it was never a one-man job: For example, the staff member who originally bought into the "going green" *concept was invaluable in managing the project's many-faceted needs.*

Dr. Susanne Lapp: *As an interim chair—my first major administrative experience—I believe that I was instrumental in effectively handling many of the details unique to the creation of an entirely new departmental presence at the college and university. To faculty, these details often appear insignificant or trifling (at best), or hotly contested and contentious (at worst). Under my guidance, the department selected its new name, and I struggled to find a respectable office where the business of running a department could take place. I created a department-dedicated secretarial pool, and led the administrative changes that come with the creation of a new department: course titling, scheduling, and numbering, beginning at the college level and continuing through to the upper levels of university administration. I led discussions on creating an image for the department through mission and vision statements, assisting and driving the accreditation processes for the department, organizing* *committees and finding representatives to staff them. Once I felt that these tasks had been successfully achieved, I decided to allow the department to select a representative from their academic area to serve as interim chair and continue the process of building the department. After about 4 years of revolving chairs, the department finally was able to search externally for a leader to take the department in the direction that it needed to go.*

In my second administrative role, as division chair of Education, the administrative position and division had been established long ago. However, I was the first "outsider" to serve as an administrator in the college's history. I personally enjoyed the role that I played in supporting tenure-track faculty within the division. I attempted to make them feel at ease (as they were moving along the tenure and promotion path) by hosting several coffee get-togethers where we would meet as a small group to talk about their teaching experiences as well as their research proposals and projects. I believe that this was a very beneficial experience for all participants.

Dr. Brian R. Clement: *Never once have I considered "achievement" as my objective. To rephrase the question: Why is "fulfillment" your foremost goal? Simple: From the time we are conceived until the time we pass, we fulfill our lives through the three-step program of passion, then purpose, then contribution. Success is the inevitable outcome.*

Vision is what successful people build their dreams upon. From a young age, I had embedded in my imagination the notion of the institute that I now have the privilege to direct. Although what has developed doesn't exactly match every specific detail I imagined, quite often the reality exceeds my fondest wish. I've allowed mental freedom to guide my decision-making, enabling an elastic approach that produces more-enduring results than the rigid variety would have. Gathering consensus from people in our organization as well as from people who are not directly involved has been fruitful—greater and deeper perspective often refines and enlarges your own potential. In a way, I picture my success as a baseball thrown at the beginning of a game. One never knows how the subsequent plays will unfold or what the score ultimately will be, yet there is boundless excitement for the challenges ahead, and the success that comes.

The three major steps of achievment (passion, purpose and contribution) all interact to create a continuous energy to implement our vision. This energy attracts the appropriate people to reach their ultimate goal and success. The creative environment at HHI fosters people to learn about themselves to become healthy.

Lavinia Lee Mears, Esq.: *The major career accomplishment I was most happy to have been involved in was saving a first-aid squad from being permanently shut down after 60 years of service. The squad had its services suspended when a large municipality improperly amended a law. I knew I could win the case for my clients, but a lengthy and expensive lawsuit would not save the squad—a legal battle* *wasn't going to solve what really was a political and public relations problem. I had to think "out of the box" to find a way to keep the squad alive.*

Instead of waiting three years for the litigation to make its way through the system, I pursued a strategy aimed at overturning the ordinance that put the squad out of business. To overturn the law, I would have to submit a legal petition signed by 4,000 registered voters in 8 days. If I could make that happen, the town would be required to hold a special election. By getting the question on the ballot, the town's residents would then be given the chance to "veto" the change in the law. A permanent answer to the squad's fate would be determined in three months, rather than three years.

I undertook the job of a petition drive, which entailed putting to use my combined knowledge of law, marketing, and public relations. I had to train, motivate, and supervise the small group of volunteers to circulate and witness the signatures of 4,000 registered voters. It was the most ambitious undertaking of my career. The squad was saved and it continues to serve the community to this day. The referendum petition drive not just was a success—it became the largest legal petition ever attempted in New Jersey's history. I had to trust my intuition (and my out-of-the-box thinking); harness the power of passion and the vision to succeed with a focused message; and motivate, unite, and inspire people around a cause despite naysayers calling our quest impossible.

3. How would you describe your relationship with your closest colleagues and people that you depended on to get the job done?

Dr. Karl K. Stevens: *I believe that we must be equal partners in the task at hand. We have to have respect and consideration for each other and each other's ideas and opinions. For example, I knew students needed a forum to voice their needs and opinions. I developed the Divisions of Engineering Student Services and Engineering Career Development to better assist and guide students in their studies, career preparation, and personal development. I feel that I have had a good working relationship with male and female colleagues, and that many of my accomplishments might never have come to pass without them. We show respect and consideration for each other's needs and continually share ideas for improving our communications.*

Dr. Susanne Lapp: *I believe that I developed my closest relationships during my second administrative experience, as the Division Chair of Education. I had the support of a wonderful mentor, the former division chair. She made herself available to me at all times and was able to coach me through difficult meetings with other administrators in the college and at the state level. Not only was she a professional mentor, but she was one of my closest friends at the* *college and we would frequently meet for lunch. Sadly, she became very ill and was no longer able to help me as much as she would have liked to, and I truly missed her support and guidance. In my first administrative experience, I was able to select a colleague with whom I had successfully worked together on other projects. Together, she and I began the heavy lifting involved in creating the new department.*

Dr. Brian R. Clement: *My relationships are transparent, honest, and clear. My colleagues are people I have learned to trust by observing and receiving their sincere thoughts and actions. There are many that articulate desires but fall short in committing themselves to them. "Birds of a feather flock together"—and, unfortunately, the great majority are talkers and not doers. Colleagues are those who share values, ethics, and, most important, honesty.*

Applying your passion will always result in success. This should be the most important lesson taught at any and all schools. Without this premise all else falters. Open discussion, candor, and willingness to change are the hallmarks of mutually beneficial relationships. Applying mentorship—as well as receiving it from those you respect—builds a stronger bond and a better personal character. In a fragile world that is too often governed by personal insecurity, egocentricity, and self-interest, it is rare to find people who are genuinely interested in enriching dialogue and purposeful progress. As a young man, my partner in my New York practice was a medical physician who had for 50 years practiced only complementary healthcare. His extraordinary perception and refined bedside manner opened my eyes to the true role of a medical practitioner. We are not meant to impose our will on those who seek out our counsel; instead, we are meant to acutely listen and respond by filling the empty spaces missing from the patient's own narrative.

Lavinia Lee Mears, Esq.: *My relationships with those people were built on mutual respect, honesty, and trust. I have been blessed to work with great people. I always tried to hire people that were the best of the best at what they do. Communication is a key to our relationship. It was important to me that everyone on my team understood the vision of the firm or the particular project. Everyone needed to understand how the project or task to which they were assigned fit into the big picture. Feedback was given consistently, constructively and respectively, always explaining the why.*

I followed the golden rule, treating the members of my team as I would like to be treated. I gave team members credit and recognized them—in front of the rest of the team and clients—for a job well done. I fostered an environment of open communication. I invited them to share their ideas for case strategies; better ways of managing office procedures; generating new business; and cutting costs. I welcomed disagreement and was grateful that my team felt comfortable making suggestions to improve upon the work I had done. I also shared the rewards of the business, giving employees bonuses whenever possible.

It was important to me to be both a gracious winner and a gracious loser. Win or lose, I congratulated my adversaries on a job well done. To me, that was what good sportsmanship required. It's no different than how my sons are taught to say "Good game!" at the end of a ball game—regardless of whether they win or lose. In cases where I felt attorneys were feeling particularly lousy about a loss, I would send them a card remarking that it was nice meeting them and complimenting them with sincerity and authenticity on their work.

4. How did you deal with stress and how did you handle conflicts with your team members?

Dr. Karl K. Stevens: *It is important to be aware of the times you are stressed. In my mind, stress arises when you don't know where you are headed. I seldom encountered this problem. I was always very fortunate to have the Universe hold up a big sign that read THIS WAY. Dealing with stress is part of life; you minimize its impact, however, if you surround yourself with a great support system. If you have the right people on the team, conflicts will be minimal and easily managed through intelligent conversation. As I got older I learned to deal with stress as being outside of myself and was able to mitigate its effects. Logic seems to combat stress—everyone can share in its calmness.*

Dr. Susanne Lapp: *There was a tremendous amount of stress associated with both administrative positions. I found that it was best to handle conflicts directly, rather than seek out protection from administrators at higher levels. Additionally, I would consistently approach all individuals with respect and kindness. I would ask individuals to meet with me and very carefully, I would listen to their comments and concerns. Together, we would find useful and productive strategies to repair damaged professional responsibilities.*

I am fortunate to work well with different personalities. I have developed a propensity for patience and the ability to

listen to what is needed. *This combination helps me resolve*
conflicts and keeps my stress level reduced.

Dr. Brian R. Clement: *Stress can be overcome when you*
use the helicopter approach: Bring perspective to the stressful
circumstance by mentally placing it within the totality of
all that you do and the objective and mission statement of
your work. Once this is achieved you recognize the issue is
temporary—only a bump on the road, not an insurmount-
able mountain to climb. "Conflicts" are merely moments
when two or more people are unwilling to compromise;
resolution is an amiable compromise, which often broadens
the possibilities.

The adage "stress is good for you" is nonsense—we know
exactly how it degrades the body and mind. The only positive
spin on stress is that it's an easy nemesis to eradicate. Stress
only afflicts me, for example, when I encounter a moment
of being unable to comprehend the circumstances I am
experiencing. But I've learned how to navigate around the
stress with a two-step process: (1) consciously relax, reducing
panic and permitting a clear view of the entirety of a situa-
tion; and, (2) try to place the stressful circumstance within
the bigger picture of life, stripping it of its power.

On my office wall, I have strategically placed a 550-mil-
lion-year-old fossil. This obtrusive stone is mere inches from
the eyes of the ill people that I counsel daily, many of whom
feel beaten and lost. I ask them to broaden their perspec-
tive and recognize that if we lived 100 years it would be

a great achievement. Comparing this snapshot in time to the 550-million-year-old trilobite often gives them pause. They recognize that their current disorder is not the gigantic monster that they built it into. That shift in perspective truly liberates one from the grips of stress.

Lavinia Lee Mears, Esq.: *Managing stress was incredibly challenging with such a demanding job. One key to a balanced life involves staying healthy by eating right, exercising, and sleeping regularly. The stress I had to manage as a prosecutor was what led me to take courses in ontology and to study at the American Yoga Academy to become a yoga teacher. I handled conflicts with my team members by talking things out and clearing the air before tensions built up. If I made a mistake or hurt someone's feelings, I would own that, apologize, and ask for forgiveness.*

While I may have owned the company, the people who ran the business day-to-day felt an equal sense of ownership. They knew I counted on them and were proud of the important part they played in the firm's operation. Most attorneys are fiercely competitive and in the heat of battle, there are times when feelings and egos get hurt. Many hold grudges. I avoided that. No matter how intense the case, I always did two things. First, I kept my sense of humor and, second, I always showed a token of respect to the attorney after the case, regardless of how contentious things had become.

5. How would you describe your career stages, and what were the major turning points that helped you reach your highest level?

Dr. Karl K. Stevens: *My academic career was quite traditional. I started as an assistant professor, and was promoted first to associate professor and then to full professor. Later I served as chair of two different departments, followed by eight years as associate dean for academic affairs and 10 years as dean, until my retirement. I was an active teacher and researcher, winning top awards in both areas, but also had a keen interest in higher education—its operation and many challenges. I have a long list of publications in both research and education, and authored two textbooks. I was fortunate to be able to "touch all the bases." Just about everything I would later need to ask and expect of my staff, I could say, "Been there, done that."*

I would say the major turning points included: (1) Being born to supportive parents that allowed me to take responsibility beyond my years—chilling to think about sometimes; (2) Growing up on a farm and in a rural community, where everyone had to pitch in to get the job done and where a man's word was his bond. If you had a conflict with a neighbor today, you had to find a reasonable way to resolve it, for he would still be your neighbor tomorrow; (3) Spending my elementary years in a one-room school, where older kids helped teach the younger ones (now a hot educational theory that goes by the moniker of "collaborative learning").

My teaching career started in the fifth grade, when I was responsible for helping students struggling with math and for giving younger kids their reading and spelling lessons; and, (4) Marrying a lady who was tremendously supportive and who had a personality that could charm birds down out of the trees. Without what I learned from her about dealing with people, I seriously doubt I could have been successful in administration.

Dr. Susanne Lapp: *I believe that I was a very eager young academic when I first decided to pursue administrative roles at these universities. I believed that academic and administrative approaches and perspectives were in desperate need of change and I quickly learned that the only way to make some changes happen was to take on the responsibility of overseeing and leading those changes. I began my administrative career with a big leap—serving as coordinator of the largest program in our department. I remained in this role for two years before being promoted to the next level, undergraduate director for the department. In this capacity I worked directly with the department chair to prepare the department for national accreditation. We successfully received this accreditation and I was once again rewarded for my participation by being appointed interim chair of a department.*

I learned a great deal in this role and looked forward to the opportunity to take these experiences to a new setting, which I did. Sadly, serving in the role of a "middle manager" in a university was not as rewarding as I had hoped it would be. I spent an incredible amount of my creative energy fighting for departmental/divisional rights while having to face increasingly complicated pressures from state and national accrediting bodies and decided that I was no longer interested in pursuing an administrative career and I have opted to return to my academic career so that I can focus on exciting and stimulating educational changes that are currently taking place in middle and secondary education.

Dr. Brian R. Clement: *Apprenticeship with hardcore, mission-oriented supervisors and friends strengthened my resolve to commit. My work is a passionate mission of self-realization. As I take each step, and reveal my own limitations, I focus efforts onto either improving my deficits or affiliating with somebody whose strengths offset them. There are no real plateaus—only a continuum of affirmative accomplishments that spur me to achieve more and experience pleasure in accomplishing my goals.*

Each morning I attempt to disassemble my previous patterns, preconceived notions, and established concepts. This helps allow me to open the doorway to new realities that can enrich my personal life as well as the work and gifts I share with others. Closed minds are the root cause of limited success. Relevance in work is only real when you are willing to grow beyond your own limits. Stories can be told about a grand plan that I had since I was a child, a plan that has been realized, step by step, through hard work—but real life is never that cut-and-dried. Life will lead you through its different stages as you are willing, ready, and capable of achieving them.

At this stage of my life I enjoy mentoring others so that they can become the best they can be by providing an open and safe environment for personal and career growth. Everyone can develop fully when they feel appreciated and acknowledged.

Lavinia Lee Mears, Esq.: *My career as a business consultant began when I worked as a public relations administrator overseeing Internal Communications at a large hospital in the metropolitan area. The training and experience I gained there built a solid foundation for the rest of my career. In addition to overseeing all internal publications for the hospital, I was trained by some of the world's most learned professionals in the areas of total quality management, crisis communications, strategic planning, and lobbying.*

Although I would have been content working in the communications field, I followed my long-term plan to become an attorney. As an assistant prosecutor, I worked long hours for little pay—yet it was the most rewarding job I ever had. The excitement of putting together and presenting a trial was like nothing I could have imagined. I had to prepare three trials a week, never knowing which would be called to go forward. The pace and adrenaline rush was akin to what I imagine stockbrokers must feel on trading floor. I was passionate about seeking justice for those who had been victims of violent crimes. Later, I opened my own firm as a solo practitioner without a single client. My tenaciousness and litigation strategies coupled with the trial experience I gained as an assistant prosecutor gave me leverage.

I practiced law on my own for seven years. I did not have the benefit of seasoned attorneys to guide me during this time, but I developed the confidence that comes with experience. Later, with a recognized and established firm behind me, my cases and successes received much more attention than they did while I had my own firm. Shortly after joining the firm, I received a number of professional awards, the most prestigious of which was being named to NJ Biz magazine's "40 under 40" list. The firm was highly respected and catered mostly to wealthy clients. Working there was when I felt I came unto my own.

6. What inspired you and how did you inspire the people who worked with you? How did people help you accomplish your goals, and how did you help them accomplish theirs?

Dr. Karl K. Stevens: *I always loved to learn—my mother had a big hand in that—and I naturally tended to hang out with those of similar ilk. Help from others typically came in the form of providing me opportunities. I enjoyed promoting and assisting in the selection of the college as home to the Southeast National Marine Renewable Research Center, focusing on developing ways of generating energy from Florida's offshore ocean currents and temperature gradients. I realized that working with like-minded people makes tasks easy to accomplish.*

One achievement I am proud of is obtaining external financial support in excess of $1 million for several highly successful scholarships and training programs for under-graduates and for K–12 students and teachers. Our future always has been in the hands of our students, and whatever support and encouragement we can give them is an investment in the future of our country.

Dr. Susanne Lapp: *I think I was most inspired when I saw that my efforts on the faculty's behalf helped them accomplish their professional goals. I was able to write supportive letters for faculty to receive sabbatical requests,*

Fulbright scholarships, promotions, and study-abroad programs. I was also able to develop and create several new university programs, all of which helped students, faculty, and the university itself. Throughout my experiences as an administrator, I relied on the help of friends that I made as a faculty member years before, as well as assistance from newly established friendships. These friends were willing to volunteer their time to help me achieve some of my administrative responsibilities and objectives.

It is important for me to be there for my friends and colleagues. We have inspired each other to reach our goals and realize our destiny. I find helping others is the key to my happiness and well-being.

Dr. Brian R. Clement: *My inspiration came from the difficult lifestyle changes that I made more than 40 years ago. The results of these changes were physical, but, to an even greater degree, emotional and mental. As I grew into a comfort zone of security, I welcomed assistance from others in building the dream and aspiration together. Solo acts are a fallacy; lasting success is impossible without joint effort. Learning is derived in my world from an endless cross-section of input. It may be from the words of John Lennon in his song "Imagine" or the speech I heard Dr. King give, or from the eyes of a newborn baby that inspires me deeply to believe that there is a God. To relegate one's inspiration to a single (or even just a few) causes would be a disservice* *to the spiritual process that we call inspiration. Freedom of heart and the abolition of filters is the surest way to allow continual inspiration to guide your heart, your soul, and your life.*

Lavinia Lee Mears, Esq.: *The person who most inspired me was Janet Rothman, my boss when I worked in health-care public relations and marketing. Janet recognized such great potential in me at the young age of 21. She encouraged me to be innovative and gave me the freedom to think outside the box. She built my confidence, supported me, and arranged for me to receive training from some of the most brilliant minds in the industry. Janet recognized my accomplishments, like a proud stage mom. I could not have asked for anyone better as a boss. When I had a team of my own to manage, I strove to emulate Janet's management style. I nurtured my team, trained them, and gave them the best support I could. Again, I followed the golden rule, kept my sense of humor, and always let my team know they were valued. They helped me accomplish my goals by sharing my passion, work ethic, and commitment to causes that were important to me.*

7. What would you like to communicate about your leadership style, experience, or where you are now?

Dr. Karl K. Stevens: *I enjoy being part of different organizations. For example I am a registered professional engineer in Florida and Ohio, and have held national and regional offices in numerous professional societies. I am a Fellow of the American Society of Mechanical Engineers. I enjoy writing and seem to be getting back to it after writing several textbooks and over 100 technical articles. I enjoyed being a principal investigator on research contracts and grants.*

I enjoy working with groups from different backgrounds; therefore, I partnered with Florida International University, in Miami, to create the Latin American and Caribbean Consortium of Engineering Institutions (LACCEI), an organization facilitating cooperative efforts in engineering education and research among member institutions. (Our college is home to LACCEI's international headquarters.) Other entrepreneurial accomplishments include my work as a founder and president of Kent Consultants, Inc., a consulting firm specializing in blast and vibration damage to structures.

As far back as I can remember, I always despised political deals and a "go-along-to-get-along" mentality. I always tried to operate openly, with honesty, integrity, and clear focus on the tasks that lay ahead. Of course, I didn't always hit the bull's-eye. I am now happily retired, living in a beautiful mountain-view home in the Durango, Colorado area that I helped design and plan, reliving my youth, banging around through the woods with my little rescue dog, Roxie. My home is "green" and is one of my great accomplishments.

Dr. Susanne Lapp: *If I ever decided to return to the role of administrator, I would make sure that faculty members understand that their departments belong to them—not the administrator. Administrators are there to help provide the structure and support, yet it is the responsibility of the faculty to come together, as a positive working unit, for the improvement, education, and success of students. As always, I believe that fair and respectful treatment of all of a department's members is crucial to the success of that department, and would do everything in my power to make certain that faculty is aware of these goals.*

I believe that everyone in my department has equal rights and should participate without fear in the decision-making process. Success is ensured when everyone shares in departmental decisions. Administrators are part of the team and share in all accomplishments.

Dr. Brian R. Clement:
There may be no single way to describe leadership, which can be framed in various contexts. One of the definitions listed in the dictionary describes it as an action of guiding or directing a group of people in an organization. Leadership

in a group of people is equal to a "cog in a wheel"; every cog has a job and each cog is equal (in its own way) to every other cog. For instance, the wheel can't turn unless every cog is in place. Leadership in this instance is a combined effort and once the group has defined jobs, they can then work together and become a team.

Maintaining truth at a focused level will inherently produce success. This success will hopefully humble you, attracting other likeminded people to be nurtured from the reservoir of honesty that reigns in such endeavors. This, too, can be a form of leadership.

Learning to communicate from your heart more than your mind is pure unadulterated motivation. Your own self-realized motive can inspire others to follow your lead—so it's important you make sure that the trail you've blazed is clear of any entrapments of expectations and anticipations. Move into all of your endeavors with an open heart and others will learn to trust you and your judgment.

Lavinia Lee Mears, Esq.: *Where I am now in life is open. An injury to my spinal cord last year virtually changed my life overnight. I spent the better part of the year in physical therapy. I was forced to my stop practicing law and focus on my recovery. For the first time, my career goals did not consume my life. What surprised me most of all? I was happy. I did not miss living life at 100 million miles an hour. I finally had time to smell the roses. I enjoyed my sons and relished being a mom without the pressures of such an intense and* *demanding job. I suddenly understood what it meant to be present. For the first time, I was living in the moment. I was no longer merely going through the motions of each day, thinking about what I needed to do to prepare for the next day. I am grateful for the opportunities my rich and rewarding career has made available to me. I do not have the "will I make it" doubts that come with the inexperience and low confidence of youth. I know that whatever I want to accomplish, I will.*

With the canvas of my professional life blank for the first time in my life, I have this rare opportunity to reinvent myself. I am excited about painting the portrait of my new life and what the future has in store. I am inspired to begin painting when I feel a cause that evokes in me passion, purpose, and peace. I have complete faith that the universe will unfold as it is intended to lead me on to that which is for the highest good.

Section Three

Bridging the Divide

"Faith is the pierless bridge
supporting what we see unto the
scene that we do not see."

"To live is so startling it leaves little
time for anything else."

"Hope is the thing with feathers that
perches in the soul, and sings the tune without
the words, and never stops at all."

—EMILY DICKINSON

AMERICAN AUTHOR AND POET

Bridges For Male/Female Leaders

The concept of a bridge has been with us since the earliest days, when our ancestors needed to cross running water or establish a connection over rough terrain. Bridges, however, not only connect distant sides of natural topography. They can also connect people to each other, or help integrate the physical, emotional, and mental aspects of an individual's self. We need to marshal not only on our strengths but also our weaknesses in order to maintain the structure of the bridges. We need to support both men and women in their quest for success and help those in distress or victimized by fear and abuse. Bridges—whether in music, land, or people—connect two different aspects so that they seamlessly flow together to become one. We are only as strong as our bridges, but they can be constructed to last forever.

Males and females often occupy opposite ends of the spectrum; they need a bridge to be able to meet in the middle or to understand the others' views. Our goal in life is to traverse the great divide between genders until it is not an issue. Metaphorical and literal bridges appear throughout poetry and literature. In music, the bridge unites two different parts of the song—the melody and the chorus. Men and women—capable of achieving comparable levels of spirituality, but different physically—can find their own kind of harmony using bridges in a similar fashion. Remember: We have to bridge our internal self, as well as self with others. The balance of power is achieved through the power of balance, which we must practice daily.

Thousands of years ago, ancient tombs called *dolmens* were marked by two stone columns connected horizontally at the top by a third stone slab—a primitive yet enduring form of bridge. Males and females working together—think of them as the two stone columns—need to build a similarly sturdy bridge to keep the energy flowing between them, enabling them to work together in creative and dynamic ways. If their columns are strong, their work can last forever. Everyone has a male and a female side; thus the bridges we rely on are not only for men and women who work with opposite genders, but also the ones that unite the individual to balance both aspects of the self. These aspects are manifested through hormonal changes and traits or personality attributes that depict general masculine or feminine behavior patterns.

PART VIII

• •

MALE VS. FEMALE LEADERSHIP

"A BRIDGE IS A SYMBOL OF STRENGTH AND CONNECTION THAT
COMBINES TWO SEPARATE IDEAS TOGETHER."

—Anonymous

Leaders face difficult decisions every day; they need a reliable method for bridging diverse opinions. Conflicts and challenges are inevitable, but a bridge can be a way to establish a meeting of the minds. Males and females working together must find a common ground—they get there by building bridges, which are vital for both genders. We see *authenticity* as a major female attribute and *boundaries* as representative of male attributes; when bridged, these support success. Solving problems requires dedication; without focus and hard work, solutions escape us. Bridges help us to cope with misunderstandings, bias, and lack of knowledge, enabling us to overcome challenges, share expertise, and pursue success. Both genders need to work together by building bridges to solve problems.

Leadership Styles

There are many different leadership styles that great leaders use, as circumstances dictate. A leader must pick the appropriate style:

- Authoritarian (strict or "bossy"),
- Consensus (all in agreement),
- Adaptive ("give-and-take," or compromise)
- Eclectic (a combination of all).

Selecting the most appropriate style in any given situation is dependent on the circumstances. At times, men or women in leadership roles can appear to be controlling or micromanaging. Women exhibiting this demeanor, however, may produce a more negative connotation than men behaving similarly. A man exerting this power is often described in a positive light, as strong or commanding. Based solely on general societal expectations, the seemingly masculine nature of the personality of wonen is deemed unacceptable. Yet we must all find a balance of our male and female sides (animus/anima). Only the people who do so are able to lead in an authentic, healthy, and balanced way.

Just as there are situations that demand "bossy" or controlling leadership, there are also circumstances that call for collaboration and constructive cooperation. An adaptive leader is more successful in accomplishing complex tasks. The secret to leadership success is eclecticism, combining different styles at appropriate times and situations. This allows intuitive and instinctual leadership to play a multifaceted role that responds to different problems or conflicts. Great leaders build teams that share responsibilities and communicate well both internally and with outsiders. Listening is immensely valuable but leaders need to take action. Actions, as the saying goes, speak louder than words. Men and women working together can—in fact, must—combine styles to be successful. When men and women act in unison the answers and foundations are stronger.

The fact that men and women are different in some ways does have various upsides. For example, the disparities can help us accept communication diversity and ease our ability to understand each other. There are many books written on this topic, including three by Deborah Tannen, a linguistics professor at Georgetown University: *He Said, She Said: Gender, Language, and Communication; You Just Don't Understand: Women and Men in Conversation;* and *That's Not What I Meant!: How Conversational Style Makes or Breaks Relationships.* Other books, such as *Men Are from Mars, Women Are from Venus,* by John Gray, also examine the miscommunication between men and women. We can bridge this gap in part by realizing that, due to the anima/animus in each person, in any given conversation or communication women can act in a supposedly masculine ways, or men in supposedly feminine ways. It is not about gender but about diversity and individuals.

Gender Conflicts

Recent research confirms that there are gender-specific differences in brain function and that the neural pathways involved are quite diverse and elaborately complex. Once our differences are identified—and the mystery resolved—we can begin to work together. We need to understand the role played by gender differences, and also to recognize that people have ways of speaking and communicating that are based on their respective backgrounds, cultures, knowledge, and experience. Gender is only an issue if viewed as such. A great leader acknowledges these differences and creates an environment for all to participate, according to each person's respective ability to communicate. An ideal environment allows all to grow, create, and participate—without regard to gender. As Eleanor Roosevelt stated on the newscast *Meet the Press* in the 1950s: "*We have not progressed at all as a nation if we are held back by gender prejudice.*" It is our job to progress, in large part by dissolving gender issues—a measure of progress that many would agree is long overdue.

Conflicts are complicated situations that leaders are expected to help resolve. Generally speaking, men like to solve problems by themselves. They do not, for example, generally like to ask for driving directions if lost. Women tend to enjoy asking questions; in fact, they often default to questions that can engage their desire to involve others—asking, for example, "*What do you think about what he said?*" They usually enjoy discussing opinions. Some women like to run away, play games, and avoid working together to solve problems; however, this is often true of men as well. It is important to be a team player; a true team doesn't fight pointlessly, but rather utilizes differences of opinion to reach a collaborative solution. Modern society and culture may prod us toward conflict, but bullying and finger-pointing wastefully consumes energy—and there is only so much energy available. If you waste it on games you get nowhere.

Political Power of Men

The United States prides itself as a progressive country, leading the world into the future. Though we are an immigrant nation with a Constitution that promotes equality, the country's founding ideals are poorly represented in our current government: One party has no females in Congress, and the other only a fractional percentage. We have never voted for a woman as president; it wasn't until Walter Mondale picked Geraldine Ferraro as a vice-presidential running mate in 1984 that there was even the possibility of a woman leading the nation. When women speak up about serious issues, male aggressors often fault them for having strong opinions. Men rarely have to endure criticism about the clothes they wear, or their hairstyles, yet this is the status quo for women in political positions. We say we prefer the substantive debate of issues over the superficial discussion of appearances, yet women must endure unwarranted scrutiny when mentioned for political office. It should be an accepted fact by now that any well-educated and passionate woman has the potential to effectively lead citizens.

The subject of sports, for example, has long provided a means of connection between leaders and those who follow them. For generations, young boys were typically the only ones indoctrinated with sports, team play, and heroic acts—the very framework of authentic leadership. But women also enjoy sports, and since the 1970s have been ensured equal opportunities for college athletic scholarships. Sports are a gateway into what had been purely a man's world; still, boundaries exist with high fences, and women have struggled to cross the loftiest barriers, especially in the corporate and political arenas. If women were to support each other, pure demographics would guarantee us most of the open legislative positions. Instead, women often compete against or even sabotage each other. If we can support each other as men do, we can accomplish great things. Men have their *"old boys' club"*; women need to foster a *"young girls' club"* of sorts.

Competition and Leadership

Generally when a man is in conflict, he is driven to win (a masculine personality trait), exiting the conflict only when he feels his heroism is guaranteed. Men feel this "competition" quite naturally, and are quick to do battle, driven to overtake their opponents, savoring the thrill of victory at all costs. Many men, of course, see women as subordinate or weak, and believe themselves to be part of the more powerful gender, naturally blessed with the strength to lead. In truth, however, anyone willing to "win at all costs" is quite weak and perhaps less intelligent than they believe themselves to be; the commitment to run around in circles, or to beat one's head against a wall, makes any worthwhile resolution unlikely. Women, by contrast, are generally known to have incredible stamina, and a willingness to seek out alternative solutions when blocked. Unfortunately, many women are as susceptible to the pitfalls of competition as men are, and have no qualms showing that masculine part of their personality. The balance of opposing forces must be achieved for harmony and success.

The Balanced Life

In ancient China the concepts of *yin* and *yang* were born around 500 BC, introducing a new philosophy about the attraction and interdependence between contrary forces such as male and female, dark and light, young and old. These forces oppose, attract, and complement, creating a dynamic of duality that is inherent in all living things. These forces must be balanced in order to avoid chaos and to enable harmony. The yin-and-yang symbol is a circle with swirling black and white aspects with a dot of the opposite in each half; this symbolizes the inherent opposite forces within each of us. Our role in life is to find a balance, not only within ourselves but with all that is around us. Competition can be a positive force if it supports others and if it doesn't act destructively; an active force must be balanced with a receptive force. These forces are at their best if they interrelate and complement each other. Partnerships with the right collaboration last forever. We should strive to surround ourselves with people who bring out the best in us so we can realize our most creative self and share it with the world.

The Benefits of Authenticity

We view authenticity as a predominantly feminine trait since women seem to readily search for the truth. Authenticity helps give us a balanced life opposing those superficial forces that surround us. In general, women's feminine traits have a greater affinity for truth than men's masculine traits do. Faced with a mystery box, men see only the challenge to open the unopened; women, generally, want to access the truth of what's inside. They want to know why it is so; they want to investigate all possibilities. Since women are now engaged in activities that men have usually excelled at, we are beginning to see a more-level playing field. For example, women playing sports will naturally develop some of the qualities and traits that help female leaders to excel: belief, confidence, attention, patience, focus, perseverance, and ultimately the competitive spirit that unites teams in pursuing goals.

Both men and women can learn from each other, in part because men naturally have a propensity to keep boundaries clear. They seem more able to separate items into categories—and place themselves in different relationships. Women see the truth in sports and tend to learn not only how to play the game, but also how to win with humility and sportsmanship. Men have always been exposed to sports. They can play games with clarity and understanding of the rules without wanting to change them. Women can learn boundaries from men and men can learn about authenticity from women. The scale can tip either way, but the balance must be maintained. We must help each other to do so.

The Benefits of Boundaries

We say that boundaries are a predominantly masculine trait because men seem to categorize and separate things more readily than women—sex and love, for example, or work and family. Boundaries, of course, show where one area ends and another begins, but they also indicate the point at which two people or things become different.

Personal boundaries can be physical, mental/emotional, or spiritual, and they help define acceptable behavior. The process of finding resolution includes acknowledging clear boundaries. Behavior and actions convey to others the nature of one's personality. Great leaders are expected to display consistent behavior, especially when it can affect their image, people, and responsibilities. Many heroic women have opted, for whatever reason, to downplay their own image, choosing to remain in the shadow of their male partners.

A person without any personal boundaries—or someone who disregards those of others—obscures, hides, or undermines their true values. It also becomes difficult to listen to others; narcissism sets in when a leader only thinks of her or his own needs. We all have some narcissistic tendencies, but only if we surrender internal control to those selfish and arrogant aspects do we lose sight of who we really are, muddling clarity of thought and making communication fuzzy. The power of self must be kept in balance.

The Eriksons' Eight Crises

An example of sustained balance—and one of history's great male-female partnerships—is that of authors Erik and Joan Erikson. They collaborated and were perhaps the quintessential couple. In the 1950 book *Childhood and Society*, Erik and Joan Erikson identified eight crises of developmental stages resulting from conflicts through our life cycles:

1) *Trust vs. Mistrust* (birth–1 yr.);

2) *Autonomy vs. Shame or Doubt* (2–3 yrs.);

3) *Initiative vs. Guilt* (3–6 yrs.);

4) *Industry vs. Inferiority* (6–12 yrs.);

5) *Identity vs. Role Confusion* (13–19 yrs.);

6) *Intimacy vs. Isolation* (20s–30s);

7) *Generativity vs. Stagnation* (40s–50s); and

8) *Integrity vs. Despair* (60s–death).

These stages expanded on the five "life stages of man" (oral, anal, phallic, latency, genital) that Sigmund Freud had introduced in the early 1900s. The Joan and Erik Erikson opposed Freud's theories of *"penis envy"* and psychosexual drives, reframing them as psychosocial drives. Growth and development, they claimed, were a result of resolving those psychosocial drives. In their description of the conflicts or crises for each stage, the relevant factor is that usually the outcome is positive and if not there is time over the course of the subsequent stages to compensate and still reach our goals.

Erik and Joan originally met in Vienna, Austria, where Joan was writing her doctoral dissertation; Erik never completed his formal education but received a psychoanalytical certificate studying with Anna Freud at the Vienna Psychoanalytic Institute.

The pair fell in love, married, and had children, settling in Boston where Erikson taught at Harvard and other schools. Joan, who was American, helped Erik improve his English, and aided in writing most of his books. Erik once noted the difficulty in separating his ideas from Joan's, since most of them, including his best-known theory on social development, evolved in collaboration with her. They co-wrote *The Life Cycle Completed* in 1987. They are the perfect example of a couple working together, incorporating the best of both worlds, male and female. We hope more couples will follow their example.

Family Challenges

There are functional and dysfunctional families, but culture and leadership inevitably start with the family unit and the relationship you have with your parents and grandparents. Role models within the family affect your sense of self, as will your relationship with any siblings. Early on, your role within the dynamics of the family will reveal itself, regardless of whether the archetype you fit is the black sheep or the hero. Because of the obvious power dynamic, early parental interactions have an outsized effect, and will likely stick with you throughout life. There can be horrible physical abuse, for example; female children (and even grown women) are often abused physically, emotionally, and/or mentally. Many of these women mitigate the situation using whatever inner strength they might have.

As part of a quest for approval, most children follow the example (or instruction) of their parents. Alice Miller (1923–2010) was a Swiss psychologist whose international best-seller, *The Drama of the Gifted Child* (1981), stated that children realize at an early age the needs of their parents and that they adapt to these needs. Basically, the behaviors of the parent or parents are later repeated in the behavior of the children, especially when those children have offspring of their own. Miller stated that the consequences of emotional or psychological abuse were more specific, insidious, and detrimental to adult behavior (more than physical, violent, or even sexual abuse). At the time, this assertion was quite sensational; most people did not discuss or try to blame parents for emotional abuse. Parents had the power and children were expected to adapt, even if the parents projected their emotional needs onto their children; children, however, can be severely victimized by such an upbringing.

Balance and Flexibility

The effort to balance work and family can be a pitfall for women. We are being raised to want gender equality, with an expectation of equal opportunity; however, even working women are still expected to be the main caretakers, raise the family, and to balance it all. Successful women suffer many consequences; even their health is affected. How can we find a healthy balance? A nanny—who takes care to avoid making waves with children—usually does not help children develop a natural sense of self. Children need to be given tasks and responsibility within their power, and their behavior evolves from the way their parents (role models) treat each other. You will treat your children the way you were treated unless you seek help or have a support system. You cannot feel sorry for yourself or feel victimized; you must overcome your situation. You have to find the strength within to pull yourself up, and put yourself in a healthy positive environment. You can be and do anything you want if the power is within you; you have to trust yourself and figure out what it is you want in life and go for it. It is never too late.

Flexibility is paramount in handling familial demands: How much power as a leader can you delegate and still feel powerful? You manage stress with your attitude, instead of creating stress for other people.

Negativity comes back to you; negative energy reflects back to you. Not eating right, not exercising, and not being happy will throw you off balance. Money cannot buy happiness; success is your definition of what can make you happy. Are you going to be able to manage your success, or will it be beyond your capability? You need routines and schedules in your life; a good balance generally equals eight hours of sleep, eight hours of work, and eight hours of play. Start off your day with balancing and scheduling your tasks; include time management. Make sure that what you plan to do is accomplished; do not procrastinate; and stick to your schedule. Your mind likes to know what you need to do next and how you are going to manage your schedule each day.

Women and Abuse

We view abuse as the imposition of physical, emotional, or mental injuries, or hurting another person. The world often portrays women as victims because they are seen as the weaker sex. But you are responsible for your own life; you must refuse to take abuse. Remember that you are not at fault; their problems are separate from you. You don't have to stay with an abusive, dysfunctional family; you can find another family, another support system, to adopt you and to provide a better role model. No matter what your family situation is, you are not merely a product of your environment; it's about *the power within*. The power within is found through your authentic self. Authenticity fosters a strong sense of self. Women have the power within them to change and to adapt from various situations including physical, emotional, or mental abuse. Recognize that you have a problem and find a solution.

A woman's beauty can be merely superficial; *authentic* beauty comes from within, shining out to your physical self. We are hoping the twenty-first century sees an end to the focus on material and superficial measures of success. Happiness means success because you will always be attracted to a positive good person. Your self-esteem and confidence comes from within. Beauty comes from within, based on exercise, eating well, and sleeping. Women have, for the last 50 years, been abusing their bodies; even those women who become sufficiently self-aware have then had to reinvent the wheel and re-learn how to love themselves. Abuse can be at the hands of another, or it can be in the form of self-abuse. In fact, *all* hurt, in the end, manifests within the self; you are the one who pays. Some women have given everything for success, at the expense of balance. Every woman needs to identify her own healthy balance and strive to keep her balance at all costs.

Women and Children

Children are a blessing, but they learn from a very young age how to play games against their parents. It's a reality that has to be addressed in a way that will support your health. If you give up everything for success, or for your children only, you will simply miss out. Technological innovation may not assure us all the answers about how to live, but we hope the twenty-first century will expand the number of options available to women. Women who are older and wiser, for example, can mentor, give guidance, and help younger women discern what is right for them. Women driven to be successful have higher expectations for themselves. Your body will eventually force you to get into balance, but will it be too late by then? This is where you pay with cancer, obesity, diabetes or other maladies. How much power do you have to have? How much can you delegate? The balance of a healthy life is the answer. When fighting the balancing act, just delegate.

Historically women have suffered abuse delivered not only by family, but also by the culture at large. In Europe, many religions, and civil gatherings separated women from men. They were considered second-class citizens, and were required to do as they were told. When society tells women they are second-class citizens, they come to believe that they are. Abuse comes in so many ways that you tend to repress it. Women's contributions and successes are not always written in the textbooks. Without the benefit of successful role models, confident levels are low, an obstacle often compounded by family dynamics. There is enormous stress on men who have to be the breadwinners. Our society requires men to be super-powerful and expects women to be subordinate. Women are required to build up men up by making them feel powerful. Authentic power—as opposed to superficial power—comes from within and requires balance. Abuse as a concept is not inherited; it's propagated through the environment. Thankfully, today's younger generation is exposed to an environment that at least aspires to equality. Contemporary children are taught to believe in equality; however, we need to ensure they stay healthy to become great leaders.

Women and Menopause

For much of our lifespan, women are fertile. As we age (35–55), nature liberates us from the burden of propagating future generations so that we can spend more quality time with ourselves. But this, too, comes at a cost: Hormone imbalances cause weight gain; researchers consistently report that when estrogen is not balanced and remains either high or low, it increases body fat in the hips and belly region.

Women who make love one to two times a week double their bodies' good estrogen. According to the Karolinska Institute in Stockholm, oxytocin that stimulates brain-cell neuroreceptors, creates endorphins which spark estrogen development. Another hormone— insulin—plays a major role in production of serotonin and helps the body repair itself, countering bodily production of adrenaline and cortisol. If we maintain adequate hormonal balance, our lives will be happier and healthier.

After menopause, progesterone (also produced in the ovaries) reverts to production in the adrenal glands. Sugar, saturated fats, and stress lower progesterone. We need progesterone to balance estrogen. Counterintuitively, testosterone is also a female hormone made in the adrenal glands and ovaries. It will decrease during menopause, yet is precipitated by pollutants, stress, birth-control pills, chemo, or depression. Exercising, losing weight, sleeping well, and taking zinc will help to increase it. We need to exercise; however, the Stanford Medical School reported that there is an increase of women's inactivity in their leisure time during the last sixteen years. Twenty years ago, 19% of women were inactive, compared to 52% now. (Men also have increased their inactivity, from 11% to 44%.) This suggests that future trends of health and exercise do not look good. We need to be more active in our latter years, not less active.

Global Health Issues

A healthy diet is important for anyone hoping to pursue a creative and productive life, especially in any kind of leadership role. As Emily Dickinson said, *"To live is so startling; it leaves little time for anything else."* Health begins in the digestive tract. The digestive tract harbors millions of bacteria per gram of intestinal content, comprising over 500 different species that have co-evolved with their hosts in a mutually beneficial relationship. These bacterial communities promote human health through effects on nutrition and immune-system development or function, so eating fiber is very important. Modern western civilization, though, has seen an increase in obesity, especially in children, due to sugary snacks and lack of exercise. Health issues should be our number one priority.

Many diseases spread throughout Europe in the middle ages, including the Black Plague, which claimed more than one-third of the population. The Protestant revolution and the doctrine of reformer Martin Luther influenced the surviving populace with regard to dedication, moral values, hard work, learning, and literacy. The industrial revolution created urban jobs; women became part of the supportive workforce, though not yet in leadership roles. Women joined the workforce as fertility decreased in southern and Eastern Europe; however, more women joined the workforce in the Western Europe, which led to the rise of modern capitalism.

Currently we are one world and one global economy; every country influences the success of every other country. New technologies enable global travel and communication, but also inextricably link every region when it comes to health. Some countries have had more than their share of health issues, and some health issues have had an outsize impact on society. In the mid-nineteenth century, for example, Ireland barely survived famine. The blight (an extinct strain of fungus) devastated the country's potato crop, leading to widespread starvation.

Female Health Issues

One devastating health issue has been smoking, which became the "in" thing to do beginning in the early part of the twentieth century. Ads for cigarette smoking were everywhere, and even though these ads often depicted such masculine imagery as cowboys on horseback, women too, smoked like chimneys. Symbolically, smoking provided many women the sense that they were now on par with their male counterparts. By midcentury, health warnings began appearing on cigarette packaging; by that time, however, many smokers were already dead or dying of cancer. Smoking-related lung cancer, emphysema, infertility problems, and other health concerns skyrocketed among the female population as well. Smoking is not only detrimental to physical health, but also affects our spiritual and emotional well-being. It is addicting and therefore removes smokers from the reality of the now. Miscarriages, weakened offspring, and reduced incomes due to illness are also connected to the inhalation of disease-causing smoke.

These are outcomes that sabotage any potential success, and behaviors that undermine would-be leaders. We seek crutches when we are out of balance; it's critical that we know we can balance ourselves simply, with the tools we already possess within ourselves. We need to know what is out of balance first, before we can adjust, adapt, and balance ourselves.

Female Leaders and Health

Women are strong by nature. As the singer Lena Horne once said, *"It's not the load that breaks you down; it's the way you carry it."* Every mother or sister carrying the load in her own way is a leader. Every woman that fulfills her wishes is a leader. Women—the ones who nurture their own strengths—make healthy choices and appropriate decisions every day of their lives. We are often the major caregivers; if our health is unstable, everything else falls apart. The family depends on women's health and balance of work, family, and self.

Our daughters, nieces, and granddaughters witness the habitual feelings and actions we display, and will follow in our footsteps, passing down whatever legacy we offer them. So if we can make choices that will keep us healthy and vibrant, we will also contribute to the future success of our families and society. Most women are leaders within their families, and many of the relevant strengths enable them to be great leaders in the business world as well—if only they had the insight to recognize it.

We are beginning to realize how important health is, and how it affects our physical, emotional, and mental domains. We have a responsibility to make sure we are healthy, not only for our own benefit, but for the benefit of others. We need to take charge of our minds, our bodies, and our lives. The easy way is rarely the right way: An antacid may ease the discomfort caused by a bad meal, but, as reported by the Kaiser Permanente Center for Total Health, people who take antacids for two years have a 65% higher risk of developing a B12 deficiency. Another problem with antacids is it can lead to stomach cancer. Males in pain are rarely deterred from intimacy, but females often turn to pain-relieving medicine. Thousands of people who take such medications end up in hospitals after overdosing; many die.

Healthy leaders seek out proactive ways of sustaining good health. Innovative human-resources executives at forward-thinking companies now encourage their employees to engage in wellness programs. Companies are researching employees' work habits and many have adopted a philosophy that tries to limit the number and duration of long meetings. (Some even rely on dance-break videos to rejuvenate workers.) In the 1970s, the food industry replaced fat with sugar and removed fiber for a longer shelf-life. Since then we have doubled our insulin production and our eating habits are out of control. Medicines such as, steroids, anti-depressants, blood sugar regulators increase insulin which is the energy storage harnone that turns sugar to fat.

PART IX

• •

STRATEGIES TO WORK TOGETHER

"I AM NOT AFRAID OF STORMS FOR
I AM LEARNING HOW TO SAIL MY SHIP."

—Louisa May Alcott

Despite society's apparent conviction that *women* and *power* make "inappropriate" bedfellows, it's undeniable that the half of the species responsible for perpetuating the entire species obviously possesses monumental strength. Humans perceive themselves to be a uniquely advanced species making consistently exceptional progress. What can we do to redress this arrogant stance, which has long been an impediment to living harmoniously within our world?

First, we must subscribe to a new form of equality that eschews existing beliefs, relying instead on our independent, authentic instincts. This equality involves accepting each gender—complete with the advantages and disadvantages of each—with the understanding that neither is "better" than the other. Working together as equals is possible; in fact, as history has shown us, some of the best partnerships have been between men and women working together.

Working together entails being patient, accepting and becoming aware of differences that are not always negative. William James was a well-known educator and philosopher who at the beginning of the 19th century said: *"Whenever you're in conflict with someone, there is one factor that can make the difference between damaging your relationship and deepening it. That factor is attitude."* Understanding and acceptance are the desired result of a good attitude, enabling us to see the problem or conflict clearly; only then can solutions emerge through collaboration.

True collaboration is only possible among equals extending each other the respect they deserve. The equality we seek involves access to equal chances and opportunities, not some myth about the respective physical capabilities of men versus women. We can solve problems together with the benefit of thoughts derived from the *yin* (feminine) and the *yang* (masculine), feelings that can blend and complement each other. This is the best of both worlds.

The Power of Collaboration

Successful and authentic leaders excel in part because they're able to note differences between team members (male *and* female) and then work together to bridge those differences. The notion of power residing primarily with males is a flawed premise; both genders are equally capable, and should therefore have equal opportunities. The highest potential for power resides in the connection and collaboration between males and females. We can accomplish great things by embracing the best of both. The saying "the whole is greater than the sum of its parts" implies that working together is synergetic and more likely to produce the desired result. Collaboration is an important key to success. Completing a task, or project, relies on the following 5 Ps:

- **Passion** for what you want to achieve—the end goal.
- **Preparation** or research in advance of the attempt—the competence required.
- **Presentation** in sharing results—the completed task.
- **Publishing** the outcome—the permanent result available for all.
- **Pursuing** some kind of follow-up—the benefit extended.

The idea and pursuit of power has led to misunderstandings, wars, and chaos. We believe, however, that power can be shared wisely—and power shared between men and women is the ideal combination. It can solve all issues. One of the ultimate exhibitions of power is the successful resolution of conflict. Each gender has a lot to contribute; the key is to work together. Building bridges between genders, ideas, and styles provides better understanding.

Embracing Differences

Since each person is a combination of male and female qualities, understanding the parts of self helps in accepting differences and building bridges to overcome them. Carl Jung described the internal conflict of the *animus* (male-self) and *anima* (female-self) within our personas. Understanding that the animus/anima conflict is universal, and that our similarities outweigh our differences, makes working together seem more reasonable. Awareness provides the opportunity to see the male and female characteristics in everyone, though societal pressure has led some people to suppress traits that diverge from what their appearance conveys. Efforts at gender inclusivity help combat this inauthenticity.

The interplay within male/female relationships is perhaps best illustrated by the ancient Greek myth of Perseus and Andromeda. The myth follows their friendship through many years of ups and downs, during which their love and compassion develops into a growing dependence, loyalty, and devotion. Passion comes and goes; what remains is a solid foundation of an authentic relationship that is based on truth and the valid, supportive actions that reinforce a partnership. Perseus and Andromeda maintained a true and trusting partnership for many years: believing in, listening to, and advising each other, absent of jealousy or suspicion.

The Conflicts of Anima/Animus

Unfortunately, we have forced modern women into an impossible position: presenting a false exterior that masks the unresolved inner conflict between their animus and anima. Recent studies show that upward of 40% of women are uncomfortable in their own bodies. This superficial self-hatred traces back to an inability to live an authentic life. Other research has shown that men have more frequent and positive views regarding sex and their own bodies, and are more comfortable with their own physicality. Men often tend to be arrogant, lacking a realistic picture of who they are. They have to reach an authentic balance of self. Women sometimes feel that they are at a disadvantage if they are not "pretty" (or, more to the point, not deemed pretty by others, usually men). Many women also define their physical attributes in relation to other women, leading to competition and envy. These feelings are due to a lack of self-esteem and the failure to develop a strong sense of self. As noted, *beauty is in the eye of the beholder.*

Every human, however, has both male and female parts of self—what the Chinese call the *yin* (feminine) and *yang* (male)—that can be tapped in daily life. When a woman is estranged from (or made to feel discomfort in) her true self, she is often awkward and unable to express her real (masculine) strong self. Multitudes of women find themselves unable to succeed merely because they do not feel comfortable in their own skin. Many are stymied by an artificial guilt centered on the notion of being unable to *"do it all"*—motherhood, domesticity, sexuality, career advancement, leadership. This not only keeps women out of positions of power, but prevents them from even seeing their own *potential* for power. Women must realize that they have choices.

Men frequently describe women in sexual terms as "conquests," but no authentic relationship can survive that formulation. In reality, men find themselves vulnerable during climax, when they open themselves to their feminine side. Men in general do not allow themselves to be vulnerable under any other circumstance. Climax is a man's only opportunity to be transparent, because his motivation for pleasure need not be obscured. At times when both partners reach climax, barriers and boundaries do not exist and a feeling of spiritual connection can be experienced; gender issues or bias can suddenly vanish. A woman's motivation for sex is also pleasure, of course, but she also yearns for a connection in a relationship, which provides her a feeling of acceptance. A mutually committed relationship provides the security a woman needs to give of herself to receive the overwhelming approval of a man.

Stereotypes and Limitations

Our society has always been affected by stereotyping and bias behavior. The overwhelming majority of women have been reduced to stereotypes. They feel obligated to explain their needs (to other women as well as men) before they feel worthy of the serious consideration of others (mostly men). We can work together to fix the current façade we call the female persona by speaking with spiritually liberated women who have succeeded in leadership by escaping categorical pigeonholes. Countless such interviews over the course of decades have provided the pleasant finding that even successful women continue to feel vulnerability, but have learned to capitalize on a willingness to express it. This openness is a good starting point for authentic dialogue. Awareness is the first step to successful change.

When a woman frees herself from artificial limitations—whether those limitations are self-imposed or have been imposed by others— she discovers an abundant reservoir of inner power. The epicenter of this power is not her brain, as she might once have believed; it resides within her exceptional heart. This heart has the strength to allow another human to be seeded in her very body, the power to give birth to this exceptional child, and ultimately the wisdom to guide this person through life. Motherhood—or even the mere potential for motherhood—is the female equivalent of Herculean strength. Additionally, each woman is hard-wired—and hormonally inclined—to embrace a partner in whom she might discover reciprocity. For some women, partnering is a formal precursor to parenting. Both genders seek out relationships of some form.

Authentic female leadership can be readily expressed when she is secure in her family, partner, friends, and offspring. Why, then, is it so hard for us all to optimize each woman's opportunities to fulfill her potential? On the female side, there is a great deal of apprehension about potential "failure"—in particular, what others may say about any woman's attempt to fully engage. On the male's side, his security may be threatened, or his power seemingly usurped, when a woman is independent enough to fully express her ideas. What is often overlooked by either side is the harsh-yet-kind reality that by supporting one another in the quest of self-realization, a woman and man can achieve two positive, secure, and transparent personas. The female/male relationship is essential for the survival of humanity. We often speak metaphorically about two halves making a whole, or even the whole being more than the sum of its parts. When opposing parts are combined, they can generate progressive results. We can have this in everyday life.

Criminal Abuse of Women

Human history includes a long and terrible legacy of female suffering: (1) Kidnapped for sex trafficking and other abuses, some locked up and tortured; (2) Victimized in sexual assaults yet accused of having "*asked for it.*" Battered by husbands or murdered by stalkers or just gone missing, having been bullied and shamed and humiliated. There may never have been a time when there *weren't* men abusing women and children at home—but physical, emotional, and mental abuse continues to afflict our society, every day, around the globe. We are bombarded daily with tales of domestic violence and atrocities inflicted upon children. Despite myriad efforts to raise global awareness—sexual offenders now must notify the communities they choose to join upon release; technology such as DNA evidence has helped curtail many repeat offenders—there is still more to do. An increasing number of safe-haven facilities now provide women some measure of safety and protection, but, again, more must be done.

Jean Baker Miller, in her 1976 book *Toward a New Psychology of Women*, believed that "*the status of women in our country has to be redefined since there are concepts that disparage and distort the basic character of women*". We know that history has shown, based on male dominance, it is easier to vilify women than to compete with them." Miller wrote that we need to show how the mental and emotional lives of individual women reflect (sometimes unfairly) the social and political system. Our goals are not unrelated: We can redefine female capabilities and expand views on authentic female leadership while continuing to highlight any instances of physical, emotional, or mental abuse that might otherwise tarnish our society.

Women and Sex

In academic institutions and corporations, the problem of gender is most acute when a position of power is used to gain sexual favors.

Most men and women in leadership roles claim that they can separate (or, at the very least, differentiate) a professional relationship and a sexual attraction—but that claim requires significant emotional maturity on both sides of the male/female relationship. We may not be slaves to physical attraction—we know the difference between work relationships and personal ones—but applications of power are often unconscious or subconscious. Men and women are equally capable of making this mistake; however, men (using the power of higher rank that they have traditionally monopolized) have typically done so in the workplace by applying sexual pressure. Women often wield their power in the bedroom by *withholding* sexual pleasure. Both are examples of the malicious application of power, and a sign of superficiality. Playing sexual games is not authentic, and deeply damaging to your strong sense of self. Even as you wield the superficial power of manipulation, you are sowing the seeds for the future erosion of that bogus power. You are behaving in a way that undermines your authentic self.

Women have been under the impression that covert power, sexual power, and manipulation of family members are authentic powers; however, we view authentic power as overt or symbolic of your true (creative) self that is available to contribute to the world. We know how important families are, for example; many women choose motherhood before pursuing career advancement. Women at work, men taking care of children, family members helping, community volunteers, nannies—we know we can't "have it all," so whatever combination works is fine. Even authentic women with clear boundaries, however, must not put their sexuality—the core of manipulation and superficial power—on display in the workplace. The political use of sexuality undermines production, limits the ability to reach goals, and subjects workers to unwanted distraction. Be who you are without regard to gender. Find the real person within, the one balancing animus/anima or the yin/yang. Just be the best you can be.

Women and Health

Society and our culture clearly do not consider women's health as high a priority as men's health. Not long ago, for example, it was revealed that women's health is on the far backburner for research money in the conquest of disease. Meanwhile, women, due to their focus on caring for others, often tend to neglect themselves. It is time that we as a society consider women's health as a major concern and help women gain knowledge and incentive to take care of their themselves, emotionally, as well as physically. Society does not yet widely recognize the holistic approach to women's health (balancing the physical, emotional, and mental aspects). Each person has to recognize their physical, emotional, and spiritual needs in order to achieve a holistic balance in their life. A balanced life allows you to succeed and be healthy.

Our global progress on this point has fallen short compared to other human advancements. Even the women's-liberation movement sparked a new layer of responsibility beyond the care of children and families. Working (a necessity in fulfilling many of us) has, in itself, given rise to diseases that are traditionally developed via stress. The historic role women had in nurturing and feeding the family has been usurped by fast food, television, and computer nannies.

This breakdown of traditional family values results in insecure and unguided children who grow into ill and dysfunctional adults. Disease rates among babies, children, and young people are outrageous—and worsening daily. No one should expect women to sacrifice their health and happiness to please others. Life should be a two-way street that brings harmony.

Women and Disease

Women generally suffer in silence—unless they take a proactive stance to insure they and their families are healthy and able to stay that way. Endometriosis, for example, is a silent disease that impairs a rising number of women each year. This disease is the result of healthy cells that form the lining of the uterus (or *endometrium*) growing and mutating outside the uterus—usually in the abdomen, pelvis, fallopian tubes, or ovaries—causing inflammation, along with enormous pain and risk of infertility. Mainstream medicine perceives endometriosis as an autoimmune disease, but it is actually a lifestyle disorder. The failure to sleep, eat, or exercise properly weakens immune-system cells, precipitating an imbalance in the homeostasis of the female system. Added to the predictable daily stress factors of life, this can create a recipe for disaster. Endometrial cancer is a form of uterine cancer—the most common cancer of the female tract, often caused by estrogen replacements, tamoxifen and other estrogen suppressors, obesity, diet, and/or alcohol consumption.

We as women are in charge of our bodies—and what goes in them. Research has found that women who ate large amounts of meat had an 80% increased risk of developing endometriosis. Conversely, those who ate a vegan diet had lowered their risk of developing endome-triosis by 40%. Caffeine consumption and exposure to PCBs and parabens are also risk factors.

HPV (human papillomavirus) is a virus with hundreds of varia-tions. It is linked to cervical cancer, which is the second-most-common cancer for women 15–34 years of age. This connection spawned a questionable new anti-HPV drug called Gardasil, targeted at teenage girls. We are witnessing human experimentation, and a generation will pass before we begin to see the real effects of Gardasil. Yes, unpro-tected sex can spread disease. But long-term use of birth-control pills, smoking, diet, and stress are also risks.

Women and Cancer

Ovarian cancer, which at one time primarily affected older women, has begun to touch females at much younger ages. One cause of this trend is unnatural hormonal disparity due to environmental estro-gens, but perhaps the root of this problem is manmade chemicals, heavy metal pollution, and unhealthy diets. (Research indicates, for example, that women who consume dairy products have a greater risk of ovarian cancer.)

Breast cancer, which attacks between one out of eight women, depending on education and cultural status, has become a plague. Over 90% of breast tumors are insulin-receptor-positive, so the amount of sugar (alcohol, bread, dairy, pasta, fruit, sodas, etc.) you eat and drink is directly linked to breast cancer. Fibroids and cysts are anatomical mechanisms that are the results of the body defend-ing itself from abnormal chemistry, infections, and toxins. Fibroids have estrogen receptors, so they grow when there is an abundance of estrogen. Fibroids thrive during pregnancy, through improper hormone treatments or when one consumes a polluted diet. Formerly, cysts were believed to be independent from cancer creation. They are now considered potential precursors to cancer. Many describe them as internal pimples, which apparently describes them in an understandable way. These growths possess the potential to complicate organ and circulatory function. For health, exercise aerobically, stretch, and lift weights, sleep and rest adequately, and make sure that your work and home environments are healthy and peaceful. Your personal relationships and the occupation that you choose absorb all of the time in your life. For this reason, it is essential that you develop a positive and strong self-identity so that you will not compromise your choices and you can handle stress.

Happiness and Lifestyle

Happier people stay healthier by living an authentic lifestyle, singing their best, breathing when exercising, and marrying the right person. Major depression can age a person's body on a cellular level, according to the University of Amsterdam. They say it accelerates aging and reverses good health. We are humans and not fruit flies (used in research), where males and females pheromones can be of detriment to them; a female having a male around reduces their fitness and the costs of courtship, mating, and offspring production is paid in higher mortality, and reduced immunity. For example, for fruit flies, just smelling rich food is enough to increase mortality rate. When male fruit flies smell female pheromones, it's enough to shorten their life. Now, that may sound familiar, but we are not fruit flies. We, as males and females, can work together through understanding and supporting each other.

According to researchers at the University of California–San Francisco, sugar contributes to around 35 million deaths globally each year. While doing brain-scan analysis, researchers found that certain foods can be addicting. Their study examined how food consumption can be controlled by dopamine contained in pleasure centers of the brain. Tania Singer, an influential social neuroscientist known around the world, showed that watching someone suffer activates some of the same brain areas as experiencing pain. It's the signature of compassion. Meanwhile, exercise creates new neurons in the brain's hippocampus, which controls short-term memory and regulates emotion by releasing GABA, a neuron-transmitter that calms anxiety. As we understand how our body works we can become healthier and more effective.

An active lifestyle improves brain health physically, intellectually, and socially. It also repairs brain myelin, the protective insulation surrounding axons, or nerve fibers. Cells release little "sacs" of proteins and genetic material into the body's fluids. Then exomes move through the body with signaling molecules that target particular cells and change their behavior. Strokes occur when blood vessels that supply oxygen and nucleates to the brain become obstructed. Besides injuring brain cells, a stroke disrupts the function of endothelial cells in the blood-brain barrier, which exacerbates brain damage. We can avoid damage to our brains by eating healthy foods, relaxing when we can with people we enjoy, and exercising which can reduce stress and ill health.

PART X

....

AUTHENTIC FEMALE LEADERSHIP

"If a gulf separates my neighbor's belief

from mine, there is always

the golden bridge of tolerance."

—Anonymous

There are clear differences between male and female leadership styles. Full success in the Jungian effort to reconcile the animus/anima sides of self requires men to tap into their female sides, and women to do the reverse, tapping into their male side. When men succeed, they are lauded for the advantage their feminine attributes bring to the table; women in similar positions are condemned for their "manliness," and considered "bossy"—or worse. The unfairness here is obvious—we all have both male *and* female parts to ourselves and men and women should have equal opportunity to deploy their fully integrated selves to maximize their likelihood of success.

Putting aside the deplorable minimization of women leaders, there are five rules—*5 Rs*—that can benefit both males and females in leadership roles:

- **Respect**—An authentic leader must not only respect his or her self but also others. Respect means the ability to see the other person as a separate entity, and to acknowledge that person's boundaries.
- **Responsibility**—Every person has to accept responsibility for his or her own actions that affect self or others. Responsibility means understanding each action and owning the consequences of all those individual actions.
- **Reinvention**—A leader must constantly adapt to sustain the interest of his or her followers. Creative and innovative reinvention allows for progress and motivation. Reinvention means to create something new from what already exists.
- **Reconnection**—A great leader must continually reach out to others. Reconnection involves multiple touching points to complete the communication or task at hand. Reconnection means to connect to a person or thing in successive efforts.
- **Representation**—A great leader inspires others through representative behavior. A leader becomes a role model and someone who inspires others. Representation means revealing the leader you are in an authentic manner.

Although men and women may have different styles and perspectives, the truth is that these differences provide a great advantage for solving problems. As we learn more about each other we can see more clearly how we are alike and how we are different. This knowledge enables us to utilize the best of both to overcome challenges without fear.

Women and a Balanced Life

A balanced life includes family, health, friends, and career. To maintain a balance, the welfare of self and others is paramount. Your personal relationships and the occupation that you choose absorb all of the time in your life. It is essential that you develop a positive and strong self-identity so that you will not compromise on your choices concerning the important decisions you make. When you find yourself in disharmonious life situations, remember that you are in control of your destiny and it is only you who can make the improvements and changes that can literally save your health and your life. Career women often refer to the balancing act of work, career, and family or home life. Our health depends on this balancing act. It is unique to each.

A woman who feels the desire to have babies must resolve an additional conflict. If unmarried, she may feel pressure to find a man to wed. She runs the risk of allowing physical or superficial needs to dominate her goals. Superficiality undermines or precludes the construction of a strong base for a relationship. Women play the game to get what they want and men play the game to get what they want. Each does whatever is deemed necessary to be seen as an attractive partner. When you have a strong self you don't have to play this game or act out. There is no need to pursue an inauthentic relationship, no need to wallow in layers of persona (sex, power, games). Relationships must be authentic and real to survive the challenges of life. An authentic leader—male or female—needs the freedom to choose which path to follow. Women need to have the chance to recognize, pursue, and fulfill their true potential with the help of—and not despite—their male or female partners.

Power through Noble Acts

A *martyr*, as defined by Webster, is a person who suffers for a cause. The Burmese leader Aung San Suu Kyi, for example, spent many years in prison to prove that dictatorship was wrong for her country and that democracy must win. John F. Kennedy, Martin Luther King, Jr., and Robert F. Kennedy are among those who died for their noble beliefs, but Aung San Suu Kyi isn't the only female martyr.

Emily Davison was a suffragette who flung herself under the king's horse at the 1913 Epsom Derby to prove that women had to vote to live. There are other martyrs such as, the more than 140 women who died in the 1911 Triangle Shirtwaist Factory fire in lower Manhattan. The factory owners made a practice of locking the women inside the building to keep them working. In the wake of the factory fire, labor laws were changed. Other women, in varying degrees, also sacrificed their freedom; for example, Princess Grace of Monaco was reported to be in an unhappy marriage and devoted her life to the arts, family, and charities. Princess Diana also had an unhappy marriage and was driven to outside love to find acceptance and fulfillment. Both died young in car crashes.

Mahatma Gandhi was another noble leader. Gandhi practiced nonviolent acts, compassion, and patience to ensure that freedom would become truth. He believed that truth stands, even if there be no public support and that peaceful means were best suited for resolving conflicts. *"I suppose leadership at one time meant muscles,"* he said, *"but today it means getting along with people.* Gandhi's life, his message, and his leadership are all symbols for the success of all. We hope his prophetic message is conveyed to both genders: Leadership once meant muscles or male dominance, and now it has changed. We have to work together.

Female Social Behavior

Understanding what young girls are taught helps us to comprehend their plights when they become grown women. Women are taught from the time they are young: *"You are the needed one, not the needy one,"* and their subsequent behavior is learned through example and reinforced by societal expectations. Some behaviors are automatic while others ask for a lot of concentration. Engaging with our environment and our feelings, we choose the behaviors that seem most beneficial; eventually they become part of our routine. The more routine a behavior becomes the less we are aware of it. It can be a trap: Habits, once formed, are hard to get rid of. Still they *can* be changed. As women we need to be aware of our thoughts and feelings, and how they translate into our actions and behavior. We acknowledge our young females behind the scenes; they have lesser egos than men. Females may prefer the *"backseat"* position, but they work more easily with others.

For many centuries women have been expected to follow social standards—standards that often centered on the subjugation of women by men. John Calvin (1509–1564), the reformer and French philosopher, allegedly viewed women as incapable, inherently evil, and complicit in Eve's guilt for having "*eaten the apple*" in the Garden of Eden. Calvin believed that men were free from that guilt and that women had to pay for their injustice to man by obeying (even being subjugated by) men. Reports suggest that Calvin at one time had more than 30 women burned at the stake after accusing them of causing a plague in 1545 via witchcraft.

Women have never deserved the corporal, mental, and emotional punishment bestowed on them throughout history; however, we are not sure that everybody believes this. Perhaps that is why women do not yet have equal rights with equal pay. We may never know the truth, but suffice to say that this has been our global heritage and we hope this will change before it is too late. Women and men have gifts to give the world and when working together, these gifts create a safe and peaceful world for all of us.

Economic Inequalities

Economic inequalities exist between men and women; this has long been a force in women's search for independence and survival. Many women stay in bad marriages simply because they cannot see themselves surviving without the income and protection of their husbands. There is overarching income inequality, of course: 95% of U.S. economic wealth is owned by 1% of the population; those born into the poorest fifth of American households have just a 7.8% chance of climbing the ladders. The reasons are social and cultural: Those at the bottom come from broken homes, crime-filled communities, and/or dysfunctional schools; no surprise, then, that they tend to get stuck at the bottom. The income gap is now twice the size of the race-based gap. Our country remains highly segregated and gay discrimination remains rampant. Women are still earning less than their male counterparts.

It is evident that the economy and women's financial status play key roles in how women make choices and their chances for feeling independent. David Barker, a physician and epidemiologist at the United Kingdom's University in Southampton believes that people are shaped inside and out by their material environment, which sustained them before they were born. Our culture just assumes that the environment works well for most people, but that's obviously impossible, since the majority of our population is women. We need to feel worthy and confident to contribute our talents and gifts to the world. Socrates (5th century BC) said, "*There is no illness of the body apart from the mind. How you think and feel changes everything; it is spiritual.*" Spirituality is above the material world and everyone is equal in that realm. We may be a product of our environment, but we are capable of overcoming prejudice, bias, and injustice.

Vision and Leadership

As women become more comfortable in leadership roles, our society will accept them as true leaders and learn to trust them. True leaders are people with great imaginations and the ability to make dreams come true. When our children are read stories, it can open a new world of vision and imagery. The leadership of mothers is natural and helps children feel strong and confident since they seem to be present when conflicts arise. Female leadership gives children confidence, support, and strength to mimic the mother's abilities. All male leaders were trained, at least in part, by their mothers. Strong families have both the mother and father as good role models. Adults who struggle without finding resolution in their lives are likely repeating behavior patterns they witnessed in their childhood homes. Respectful fathers, strong and free-thinking mothers, and transparent communication manifest happy, healthy, and productive children. This may be a utopian and ideal view of the nuclear family, but it's also a reliable framework in the creation of future leaders. There are many who grew up in dysfunction, discord, and even violence. They have brought about their own renewal by working on their emotional parts of self. In either case, our perception of what either did or should have happened can manifest the strength, focus, and vision to lead others.

The ability to lead is not a gift; it is a learned experience. *Listening* is leading. *Loving* is leading. *Allowing* is leading. Hierarchical models that prevent expression and demand production ultimately fail, and good leaders never utilize these broken techniques. All of this simply comes down to self-realized people, who trust that they do have the wherewithal to nurture, support, and assist others in acquiring the same. We are all so used to being barked at that when we are kissed we think of it as a sign of weakness. We should now banish the male-dominated persona of *strength through disregard* and replace it with *strength through love*. When this occurs, women will take their rightful places among the leadership elite and permit themselves to authentically express their deepest feelings without being accused of being delicate. The people we admire are always people possessing candor, transparency, and truthful expression. When we are happy in our own skin, we can support others in being happy in theirs.

Culture and Behavior

Cultural indoctrination has portrayed women as dainty non-contributors who should always take the backseat and be subordinate or covert. This grievous misunderstanding somehow ignores the fact that women perpetuate our species by not only by giving birth to us all, but caring for us. In addition, women's capacity for compassion, understanding, and character-building generally far exceeds that of their male counterparts. Negligent are those who do not acknowledge the powerful and central role that women play in the human experience, and yet few global communities have significantly addressed the victimization of women. Chinese culture, for example, continued to embrace the foot-binding of young girls until 1949, and many African countries still surgically remove clitorises under the auspices of religious rituals. In the Western culture, bras, short skirts, and high heels—all inventions to please men—are accepted as normal, even though they ultimately deform female physiques. Much of what is considered matter-of-fact when it comes to the female population is, in fact, oppressive. In what we call the number-one country in the world—the United States—most women's salaries are 20% less than those of men, although study after study reveals that their productivity generally exceeds that of men.

Many parents seem to teach their boys that they are the center of the universe, or at least the kings of the household. The lessons take root early and last a lifetime. In the bedroom, women are expected to take birth-control pills, wear IUDs, and employ hormonal patches, as well as utilize "post-romance" foams. On the other hand, males generally are annoyed when asked merely to use a prophylactic. Since the onset of regulation and oversight, pharmaceutical products have been researched and tested before distribution to the general public. These animal and human studies, however, have often purposely excluded female subjects, in the fear that the terrain of higher hormones might skew the findings and drug companies' desired results. This means that practically 100% of the medicines on the market (or at least their recommended dosages) are not appropriate or even wrong for more than half of the human population. (We now realize that even the birth-control pill has serious adverse effects.) There is a way that this can be corrected. We have to be aware and take action.

Countless examples of unconscious and conscious disregard and abuse of women plague humanity. There is a brazen inequality, for example, between female and male sexual experiences: Males are expected to have pleasure and females are their conquests.

Current Female Leaders

In the far-too-recent past, women were not permitted to vote because they were deemed "too emotional" and men feared women would be unable to make such an important choice. Once again there was a blatant bias that proved erroneous; however, things are beginning to change. Today, we are still seeing many firsts for women—the first female CEOs of major corporations, the first female Speaker of the House of Representatives, and maybe soon the first female President of the United States. You would almost think a new creature had arrived on Earth, one finally able to match the accomplishments of the human elite (most of whom have been men). Accomplished women, in short, are making their mark:

- **Marie Crandall, MD, MPH**, is a teaching professor at Northwestern Medical Group, specializing in trauma and emergency surgery. Dr. Crandall, an activist, triathlete, and vegan, is collaborating with several researchers to expand urban trauma centers in Chicago. She is affiliated with Northwestern Memorial Hospital and lobbies for the creation of more trauma centers to help those afflicted with gunshots or domestic abuse. She is determined to make a difference by caring for the needy.

- **Dr. Kalynda Gonzales**, a neuroscientist who is recognized for her advanced research in Boston. Gonzales, who received the Ronald E. McNair post-baccalaureate achievement award from The University of Massachusetts, is now a postdoctoral scholar at Columbia University doing brain research on the basal ganglia, which is responsible for tremors and has been gauged abnormal in patients suffering from Parkinson's and Huntington's diseases. Her work is ground breaking and adds to potential cures.

- **Helen (Heidi) D. Reavis, Esq.**, is managing partner in the New York City law firm of Reavis, Parent, Lehrer LLP, where she is also head of the firm's Employment and Discrimination Practice. She is a graduate (with honors) from Smith College and the University of Chicago Law School. She also has received a graduate certificate from the University of Lund, in Sweden. Reavis has served on the board of many organizations, including: The Women's City Club of New York, Women Make Movies, Women's Forum, and the Friends Seminary School. She makes a difference in her community, city, and the world as an advocate and role model for female leadership; her lectures at various institutions are a mark of her dedication. She has also collaborated with her husband Steve M. Engel on documentary films and won an Emmy Award (among others) for their film *A Walk to Beautiful*. That film depicts the horrors faced by women in developing countries who suffer from Obstetric Fibula, a condition resulting from obstructed labor if a C-section is not available in communities lacking maternal health care.

The following are Heidi's views on leadership:

1. What axiom do you feel is the secret to your success, the most important mantra in keeping your leadership unique?

I try to ignore the competition and push back when told that I cannot succeed. This instinct is ingrained, a reflection of what an ancestor of mine was told years ago by Abraham Lincoln: "Always bear in mind that your own resolution to succeed is more important than any other one thing." [letter from Abraham Lincoln to Isham Reavis, November 5, 1855]

2. What accomplishments are you most proud to have been part of, and how did you achieve these successes?

My husband Steven M. Engel and I produced the documentary film A Walk to Beautiful, on the subject of obstetric fistula, a medical condition afflicting millions of women worldwide. The condition is the byproduct of an obstructed birth—when a Caesarian section is required but the pregnant woman is unaware. This leads to the death of the baby, and in many cases the mother dies as well, or else suffers internal tears that lead to a lifetime of misery and being an outcast as women with obstetric fistula leak blood, urine, and/or feces. We funded the film ourselves and hoped for co-funding from others. We maintained our vision of the film, which in the end was featured in more than 35 film festivals, won the IDA Best Documentary Award and many other coveted awards, including an Emmy Award for the film's television version.

3. How would you describe your relationships with your closest colleagues, and with the people that you depended on to get the job done?

My relationships are co-reliant. We work in partnership with everyone at every level.

4. How did you deal with stress and how did you handle conflicts with your team members?

I try to be open and regular in communications—both positive and negative. I try to keep the negative part constructive, and expect the same from everyone.

5. How would you describe your career stages, and what were the major turning points that helped you reach your highest level?

Being passionate about a field and working at it for many years leads to having a strong reputation in that field. Turning points in my career came when I decided to form my own law firm around 20 years ago, reorganized the firm around 10 years ago when one of our partners showed great hostility to other partners, and then over time becoming more academically interested in my field of employment law. I have always had a very supportive husband and we have a highly functional partnership together.

6. What inspired you and how did you inspire the people who worked with you? How did people help you accomplish your goals, and how did you help them accomplish theirs?

I have always urged colleagues to explore what interests them most, find out where their passions lie, and figure out how that passion can be applied to their work. To see what they do not as a job but a passion. Additionally, the firm engages in some public interest and other types of creative work as a whole, so all of our personnel feel a part of that.

7. What would you like to communicate about your leadership style, experience, or where you are now?

I believe I am known as someone who is not above anything, and relates well to people of every walk of life. I urge our colleagues to emulate that, and find that the ones who do are more successful. Billie Jean King's words—"champions adapt"—are important. People need to roll with the world and not plan too far ahead or be crushed by what they cannot change. Humor helps, and having pragmatic friends or family you can speak with honestly. I also believe there are two types of people: producers or consumers. I prefer and have more respect for the former.

Women and Equality

Women's allure is well accepted by men, yet when the apple doesn't taste the way they expected it to, they blame the woman for seduction. How many times do we have to blame women for any injustice or loss? Can we at least attempt to create some real equality? Real men respect and honor the contribution women make. Unfortunately, the masses of insecure men fear women for their inherent power and strength. They misspend their energy on suppressing more than half the world's population. Until men trust themselves and feel (and demonstrate) authenticity, they cannot trust others, including their own wives, mothers, or daughters. Cancer is widespread, yet a more pervasive cancer is that of women's oppression.

The Forgotten Female Leaders

For 500 years, Europe has had women rulers who have made their mark on history. Queen Elizabeth I said in 1588 at a camp with her troops during the battle against the Spanish: *"I know I have the body of a weak and feeble woman; but I have the heart and stomach of a king, and a King of England."* She was defending her female leadership; winning the battle fostered great pride and nationalism in England. We all can identify with both her great courage and her angst, having to prove she could be a great leader "despite" being female. She became an example of strength and courage for future female leaders. If we can acknowledge we are not men but can fight as well as they do, with comparable strength of character in battle, then we all win.

Our ancestors landed in America in the 1600s to "form a new nation with freedom for all." When they arrived, they encountered a different culture foreign to their own, that of the indigenous people of America—what we've come to call Native Americans, comprising hundreds of separate tribes. Like the many countries and regions of

Europe, each Native American tribe had its own culture, language, identity, beliefs, political structures, and customs; however, they all revered their elders—women as well as men—who became their advisors.

The tribes may have had many differences, but generally Native American women were regarded as equals to men (at least prior to contact with European settlers). In some ways, they were regarded as more powerful than male tribe members. Indeed, the greatest compliment that could be paid to a young brave was that *"he is as wise as an old woman."* Despite the important role of Native American women in history, the pages of textbooks and the frameworks of classroom discussions continue to overlook their many contributions.

When Europeans first arrived in the Americas, Native American women had more authority and autonomy than women in Europe did at the time. Viewed as sacred creators who sustained their people with their life-giving ability to birth children, women were revered by their tribes. Women wielded great political, social, and economic power in pre-European America. Clan matrons chose which men would be the tribe's chiefs and had the power to remove chiefs that displeased them. In contrast to the patriarchal societies of European culture, where women took their husbands' names and men acquired all property rights, Native American clan membership and property descended along matriarchal lines. Women held prominence, and with good reason.

Native American Women's Work

Women also had much more responsibility than their European counterparts had, performing what many Europeans considered to be men's work. While tribal men's duties were limited mostly to hunting, fishing, and fighting, women were responsible for managing virtually all aspects of the community, including farming the land. (European women, it should be noted, were entrusted with spinning, weaving, churning, making cheese, and brewing ale—hardly insignificant tasks, but definitively seen as "women's work.") The European incursion into North America effectively diminished the power of Native American women, mostly due to cultural assimilation. European settlers would only negotiate in trade with Native American men. Despite the damage to their authority, Native American women continued to be powerful members of their respective tribes. Today, women lead nearly one-quarter of the nation's 562 federally recognized Native American tribes.

Notable Native American Women

For the early European settlers, life in the new world was difficult in the extreme. The conditions were harsh, rendering invaluable the assistance of Native American women—none more so than that of Pocahontas and Sacajawea, the two best-known Native American women to have aided the colonists.

A romanticized figure in American pop culture and history, Princess Pocahontas (1595–1617) is best known for saving the life of colonist John Smith from the wrath of her father, Chief Powhatan, in 1607. Just 12 years old at the time, and in the face of the resentment most Native Americans felt toward the interlopers, Pocahontas learned English and became an intermediary for her people. She built an enduring relationship with Jamestown's settlers, traveling there often to deliver messages on behalf of her father and exchanging food and supplies; she also negotiated the release of several Native Americans held as prisoners by the English. In 1616, Pocahontas voyaged to England to promote colonial interest—a goal she achieved by captivating the English royalty and generating publicity that raised awareness of the colonial settlement. We owe the success of the colony at least in part to her ability to communicate with (and gain the friendship of) possible enemies.

Sacajawea (1788–1812) was a member of the tribe now known as the Lemhi Shoshone. She was six months pregnant when she joined Meriwether Lewis and William Clark in their expedition of the United States' newly acquired western territory. Acting as an interpreter and guide between 1804 and 1806, Sacajawea proved invaluable to the safety of the expedition during its arduous journey of thousands of miles to the Pacific Ocean. Tribes that the expedition encountered en route were put at ease by the high-profile presence of a Native American woman, communicating the peaceful intent of the mission—a message made even more clear after Sacajawea's son was born in February 1805, while the expedition wintered at Fort Mandan. Lewis and Clark also allowed Sacajawea to vote in all decisions, a privilege that inspired the women's suffrage movement of the early twentieth century to embrace Sacajawea as a heroic and iconic symbol of women's worth and independence. In 2000, the United States Mint issued the Sacajawea dollar coin (depicting Sacajawea and son Jean Baptiste). In 2001, as one of the final acts of his presidency, Bill Clinton gave Sacajawea the title of Honorary Sergeant, Regular Army.

Contributions of Native American Women

Queen Alliquippa (c. 1670–c. 1700)	Known as "the Queen of the Delawares," and a leader of the Seneca tribe near Pittsburgh, Pa., she was a powerful British ally instrumental in starting the French and Indian War; Major George Washington met her, as did most who traveled through her territory; received great respect from white explorers.
Madame Montour (c. 1684–c. 1752)	Interpreter for British in Philadelphia between the Iroquois and New York Governor
Nancy Ward (born Nanye'hi) (c. 1738–1822)	Led Cherokee tribe to victory and headed Woman's Council & member of Chief's Council
Princess Angeline (1820–1896)	Eldest daughter of Chief Seattle became the unofficial ambassador for Native American rights simply by standing her ground
Eliza Burton "Lyda" Conley (c. 1869–1946)	First Native/European Indian to be admitted to bar in Kansas and argued in Supreme Court
LaDonna Harris (1931–present)	Comanche who founded Americans for Indian Opportunity (AIO), a multi-tribal organization that helps provide new opportunities; Comanche (hunter-gatherers of the southern plains) were known for the great horse skills of their men and the great inner strength of their women.
Wilma Mankiller (1945–2010)	Principal Chief of the Cherokee Nation; lobbied federal government to improve health care, education, and civil rights
Cecelia Fire Thunder (Lakota) (1946–present)	Oglala Lakota tribe's first woman president; activist for women's rights

| Winona LaDuke (Anishinaabe) (1959–present) | Two-time U.S. vice-presidential nominee of the Green Party; activist and author of three books, including the novel *Last Standing Woman*; named Woman of the Year by Ms. Magazine in 1997; inducted into the National Women's Hall of Fame in 2007 |
| Cassandra Manuelito-Kerkvliet (Diné) | The first Native American woman president of a mainstream university (Seattle's Antioch University, 2007–2013) |

There are many more Native American women who contributed (or continue to contribute) to society without sacrificing their heritage. These women have made their mark in history and we hope that our education system begins to afford their accomplishments the appropriate recognition. It is no understatement to say that we are all here in part because of them.

Women and Success

In the pre-industrial age, the masses were agricultural and self-reliant. Money was seldom used, with trade for goods far more commonplace. Steam engines in the eighteenth century powered a new way of thinking, and by the mid-nineteenth century Britain had sparked the Industrial Revolution in earnest, with assembly-line manufacturing.

The aristocracy saw its newly developed factories as machines for gathering greater wealth. Their first hurdle was to convince farmers to abandon their familiar surroundings and livelihoods. Living off the land, of course, was what humans had done from the dawn of time. Promised the excitement of the big city, the poor farmers and their families were often led to filthy ghetto dwellings in industrial cities. Workers realized soon after losing their farms that the additional monies they made were merely redirected toward paying rent and purchasing food. The majority of homemakers become more distraught as time passed.

Industrial leaders were not content with the windfall profits they were making off the sweat of others; they then created corporations. As decades passed, some of these became multinational entities, and eventually mega-corporations became the norm. The inevitable outcome of what began hundreds of years ago is reflected today in the most basic statistics: In the United States, as well as in most developed countries, a handful of people control the overwhelming majority of the economic wealth. The middle class, born out of industry, is rapidly dwindling as money moves upward at an ever-increasing speed. Greed has become a religion. Women in leadership positions, however—as CEOs and politicians—might be able to change the course.

Cultural Revolution

After the industrial revolution, women found themselves in jobs that was previously allocated to men. To succeed in a corporate environment, women often must go against their innate maternal instincts to become the disconnected, angry, and self-involved individuals they've seen succeed before them. By accommodating the alleged requirements for success, these women are paying the price—with their health. Professional women have not yet achieved equality in earning potential, but health statistics reveal the only equality they *have* earned by living in this overzealous, angry, male-dominated society: disease equality. Illness is winning in the battle over work-ing women's health, extending the list of defeats we must overcome: defeats of our individuality, of our creative spirit, and of our family units.

Industry and corporations essentially disregarded women as seri-ous employees until World War II, when labor shortages required an expansion of the female share of the workforce. Later analysis of the operational results showed that females performed better across the board than the males they were replacing had. This convinced the corporate and industrial elite they had the justification to embrace women in the workplace—effectively doubling the economy of the world. What a dilemma then, in the postwar years, after sending these wartime workers back to their baby-boom homes, to convince child-loving, nest-feathering housewives they should abandon their families for the sake of a few dollars. As the 1960s arrived, however, so too did a generation eager to remake the landscape.

Madison Avenue and its wealthy allies fashioned a message that successfully led women to believe they could gain success and power simply by emulating men. Even the women's movement seems to have been confused. Rather than asking for respect for their feminine persona, they agreed to play the role of men to gain that respect. Although women should have the prerogative to do anything they wish, concrete roles and stereotypical examples reign. Many single corporate women state they wish they had a family and a committed relationship. Sadly today to economically survive, most households require both the husband and wife to be fully employed. In many ways, we do not *want* to turn back; now, however, we don't even have the option. What we *can* do is move forward with a new agenda to change the future. We must remember the balance of power can shift and the power within balance gives us freedom.

Succeeding at Success

As men and women attempting to work together, building bridges toward common ground, we need first to understand the possible differences between us, and how to reorient them to our advantage. What prevents a woman from accomplishing major feats, or achieving a position of authentic leadership? Fear of *putting herself out there*? Fear of success? Does she fear failing to gain (or, worse, fear losing) approval from men or society? No doubt some combination of these baseless fears, and others. These fears, however, are not real. They're merely a reflection of what society has taught women to be afraid of—the fear of not being loved or wanted.

We, as women, need to remember we do not have to be perfect; we just have to try to succeed. Winston Churchill was perhaps the most eloquent on the link between success and failure: *"Success is not final; failure is not fatal; it is the courage to continue that counts.... Success consists of going from failure to failure without loss of enthusiasm."* We need to be a marshal of our own enthusiasms, and remain courageous in the fight for what we believe in. As women we know we had the power twenty-five hundred years ago and maybe it is time to shift the balance of power. The shift will bring out the best in all of us. We just want to share.

Highly successful women have a hard time coping with success. Lacking a strong sense of self, men in leadership roles (and occasionally women, too) can become bullies or put others down. This is a hallmark of insecurity, which manifests among those who have reached positions of power without authentically earning their status. The *Napoleon Complex*, for example, describes men of small stature who believe their (lack of) height requires an overcompensation to prove their worth: bullying and belittling those around them. Highly attractive female executives often fall victim to a similar overcompensation, believing that others view them as inadequately capable of fulfilling the requirements of their positions. We need to accept each other regardless of physical attributes, earning respect based on ability, mental and emotional prowess, and on achievement. Only then can we succeed in solving problems and leading others to success. Working together gives us more power than *going it alone*. We cannot give these fear complexes power over our ability to succeed. We can be balanced. We have the know-how, the motivation, the dedication, and the ability to build our bridge of unification.

The formula for success is to understand fully the balance of power and the power of balance. We need to focus on the greatness of people. Women can do more than merely contribute; they can be authentic leaders. We hope to inspire you to find your authentic calling, and to pursue it without fear. We are here to help and remind you that you are not alone.

About the Authors

DR. KATHERINE C. POWELL

Live with truth—authentically;
Value curiosity, adventure, and justice will follow

Once I begin something, I embrace it. At age 2, I was a dancer; by 4, I was leading other little girls during recitals. I have been a dancer all my life. I participated as a pro-am competitor in international Latin ballroom competitions and cofounded an argentine tango school in Buenos Aires. I am accepted as a leader in all the projects that I have participated.

I was born curious. I always figured things out by taking them apart and putting them back together—though not necessarily the same way. At age 5 I loved working with wood and I made myself an electromagnetic telegraph. It was an open wooden box with a metal hinge; the top nail had wire around it attached to a battery; when connected, the hinge would hit the top nail making a noise. This was fun—and the first step in a life of making connections that matter.

I've always been involved in connections and communication. Inspired by the secret codes from 1950s kids' shows and movie serials, my next-door neighbor and I connected two cans with string so we could talk between our windows. I also love adventure and I am never bored. When I turned 7, my father gave me a chemistry set, which I used to create fire water (invisible ink) with sulfur, water, and other chemicals; a lit match would reveal what I'd written. At age 12, my Dad gave me a typewriter, the beginning of my new world. I've never changed: I still want to reveal hidden truths and do adventurous projects.

Adventure also meant loving nature. I made a fishing pole out of bamboo, and I'd make my mom cook whatever fish I caught. I would find snakes and bring them to show her: "*Look what I caught!*" I was always inquisitive, looking at bugs and frogs; my favorite playtime was looking at the ant village I'd built. This was how I spent my childhood, looking for adventure.

My brother Jerry, who is five years older, had a lot of toys, which he shared generously: model planes, cars, and boats. I played with his Lionel train set, constructing an entire village; I love projects and enjoyed his erector set by building things and inventing gadgets. I was an athletic tomboy and spent time racing on the street with boys, playing "catch me" games to prove I was as good or as fast as they were. I also loved all kinds of games. I'd play Monopoly for days and loved Scrabble. My mom taught me how to play canasta by the age of 9 and I enjoyed all the card games she'd play with her friends. I also had fun putting on comedy shows, imitating famous singers of the time, and making the neighborhood kids laugh.

My parents were such different people: Dad was strict and mom was a yenta constantly pushing me to go out and have boyfriends. I knew by 12 that I was going to be a virgin until I finished college; I wanted my college degree and I wanted freedom. I recall sitting on my bed at 16, pounding the pillow and screaming, "*I'm going to be INDEPENDENT.*" My goal was to be on my own; clearly I wanted my own money and a career.

My mother and brother had a very close relationship, but I always felt like an outcast. Two important connections saved me: the one I shared with my father, even though he was working all the time, and one with Thea Artemis, my mom's second cousin.

Thea Artemis had a house in New London, CT, where I would stay each summer, and a place in New York City, where I'd go during school vacations. She had two daughters (Thetis and Diana, whom I love and admire), and she always told me I was her third daughter. That was lucky for me, since I was eager to escape my home life. To this day, I still enjoy visiting my cousins JoAnn, George, Diana, Roy, Heidi, Steve, Cynthia, Bill, Andrew, Ellen, Matt, and their families in the New York area, where we gather at a Greek gourmet restaurant. I love to go to Greece, where my first cousin Efi lives (our moms were sisters). I've always loved visiting Efi and her family—today she has a son (Nikola), a daughter (Dimitra), three granddaughters, and a dog. I love my friends (both male and female) who are a wonderful support system providing love and joy in my life.

I went to college at Syracuse University, where I majored in bio-chemistry and minored in French, spending my junior year studying at Poitier University in France. My facility with languages helped me land a job at the United Nations in New York City. after I was working as an assistant for the BBC's correspondent, attending press confer-ences and translating news around the world. While at the U.N., I fell in love with my future husband Bogomir (now deceased), who also worked there; he thought I could triple my salary by working with computers. He was right, of course, and he supported me through everything. He would work all day and go to school at night, while I also worked, cooked, and cleaned in the evening. I guess I did it all except for having children.

Computer technology connected me to the next stage of my career. I landed a job at Nabisco, where I became a manager after a couple of years. I soon became the second woman in the history of the company's Manpower Management Orientation program to earn a top-level executive position—a slot they could only call "computer database expert" since not many people knew what I knew. I was extremely successful, earning a six-figure salary eventually—a rarity for women in that era. In the 1980s, I started (Inter-Active Management) my own consultancy business, making $500 for a few hours as an efficiency expert, ferried to meetings in the limousines of CEOs. As deregulation, auditing, and compliance protocols were upending corporate America, I was regarded as *a woman in demand, with unique analytical and perceptive skills.*

Unfortunately, as a successful executive woman in the 1970s and '80s I would suffer my share of sexual harassment, which in those days was not acknowledged, let alone compensated for which led me to question my status. I had enough of "money" and "titles" and in the 1990s I knew I was destined for something more meaningful; therefore, I left NYC and went to school to get a master's degree in psychology at Boston College. I wrote my master's thesis about adolescent girls with emphasis on conflicts and career choices. (After transforming that into a well-received paper on adolescent identity issues, I presented it in the 2012 symposium in Athens, Greece.) I was encouraged to go for my doctorate. (A well-known Boston behavioral psychologist mentored me to become a developmental psychologist; much to my surprise, he predicted I would write many books.) For my doctorate at the University of Massachusetts at Amherst, I studied conflict management, life cycles, developmental psychology, and social justice. My dissertation was on developmental challenges and barriers of senior executive women and their coping mechanisms. Later on, my paper on gender issues was published after my presentation at Oxford University, England, in the summer of 2010.

For three decades, my days had been filled with mental stress, with very little social contact aside from a staff that I'd trained to concentrate on work. I felt responsible for the projects I had, and we were a team. I never missed a day; all my projects were done on time and under budget. Still, I found I needed to balance myself. Ten hours a day, I was a high-powered executive; by night I was an artist, dancer, and creative entrepreneur. I played guitar, keyboard, percussion, and bass guitar; a four-track studio in my apartment enabled me to turn my poetry into songs that were published locally. In New York City I would dance at Luigi's Jazz dance studio at night. I would take singing, aikido, and acting classes in my spare time on weekends. In Boston, I studied mime (acting and dance), as well as international folk dancing (which I also taught on Sundays at MIT). I met students from all over the world. My life is never boring.

After I finished school, I took off for the Virgin Islands in 2000, where I was a consultant at the University of the Virgin Islands developing online courses. I also taught at private high schools and was a guidance counselor. I had several other part-time jobs (a tour guide and I worked in the bookstore that I planned to buy). During three years there, I danced at all the island parties, started a singles club, and volunteered for the battered-women's home, helping young women to feel confident by teaching them to manage their self-esteem. The best part of the adventure, though, was the freedom to go snorkeling every day. I felt free and healthy.

In 2003, I applied for a job at Florida Atlantic University, where I served first as an adjunct professor for a year and then full-time for 10 years, teaching educational physiology until 2014 when I decided to retire and become an adjunct professor again.

In the current stage of my career, in addition to being a consultant I have also become an author. I wrote textbooks in 2006 and 2012 about teaching and learning educational psychology, and I am currently co-writing a literacy text. I've also written books with each of the directors of Hippocrates Health Institute, Dr. Brian Clement (*Belief: Integrity in Relationships*) and Dr. Anna Maria Clement (*The Power of a Woman: Leading the Way*). It has been an honor and privilege to work with them during these past few years.

Going forward, I plan to continue my travels and figure out why life, during the 6th century BC, was great for both men and women, with none of the gender issues we face today. People traded all along the coast of the Mediterranean Sea during the centuries prior to 500 BC. They bartered rather than paying with money which helped people to connect, respect each other, and not cheat, since it was not about money, but need. Money is like time; both don't exist, they are relative concepts no absolute. The ancients kept peace and harmony since they were interdependent. There was love since each person was considered a gift (one with nature) as depicted in their paintings and murals. No major wars occured until the Persians started expanding their empire in the 5th century BC by invading Greece. Coins were invented around 500 BC to 400 BC in Asia Minor and spread via the

Roman Empire. Hoarding money became a pastime; therefore, greed, wars, and empire-building initated a shift in power where women's rights became curtailed.

I will spend the rest of my life trying to find the answers. I believe we can reintroduce into our lives that joy, happiness, love, freedom, and harmony with nature. The balance of power always shifts. Love is always there. Peace is around the corner. Here are my responses to three of the questions which we asked:

What accomplishments are you most proud to have been part of, and how did you achieve these successes?

The most significant was a huge computer project I led. I had a design team of five men who were online-transactions experts, and we had to decide between two designs. The two men who presented the ideas were fighting head on. Neither would budge, and each thought that the other should give in. I couldn't fire either of them—I needed them to do the job—so I developed a strategy. I thanked them both for their brilliant work, saying how great each design was and accepting each as a possible solution, but that we had to pick one as a team. I reiterated what had to get done, the parameters, and our restrictions; then I asked them what they thought. By fostering collaboration, I helped them finally agree on one solution, which we finished on time, with smiles all around. I will never forget how amazing this was; an exercise in tolerance.

How would you describe your relationship with your closest colleagues and people that you depended on to get the job done?

My relationship is one of respect and high regard for every person no matter what their titles or jobs. Each member of a team is an equal and I make sure everyone is appreciated without having favorites or unfair rewards—all get accolades and praise when deserved. I like to feel we are a family and we can only succeed if each one of us is happy and feels important. We are a team and that is the way it works. Anything else spells disaster, with targets missed and budgets blown. The last ingredient is humor—laughter and having fun. That is the key to any successful team; if everyone is happy then it is not work but enjoyment.

How did you deal with stress and how did you handle conflicts with your team members?

The mind (cognitive), heart (emotional), and body (physical) parts of self all have to be in balance. I needed to do things at night to offset the stress of my mentally exhausting day. I've always been happy singing and dancing and acting, but my main way to relieve stress was to dance. I've been an international Latin ballroom pro-am competitor, and I co-founded an Argentine tango school in Buenos Aires (for underprivileged teens). I also did yoga and Aikido for fun and when I lived in New York City I would walk all over town—sheer joy. I joined a gym to swim and play squash (to compete in amateur matches). I was mentally, emotionally, and physically active. I have adopted Theodore Roosevelt's motto that any ACTION, right or wrong, is better than doing nothing. I hope to have a more active and healthy life-style again. My retirement will give me that chance.

DR. ANNA MARIA CLEMENT

You don't choose your calling;
Your calling chooses you—and you can't quit it.

I had the privilege of being born in a rural town in Sweden, a socially advanced country with a down to earth atmosphere. This gave me a practical outlook about health and well-being. My family provided a secure home and the freedom to explore my interests—a life created for me as a *gift of love.* This safety and feeling of belonging has always been with me wherever I am and whatever situation I encounter. My stable and structural childhood consistently supports my personality of strength, patience, and leadership.

My dad was an entrepreneur and my mom was a housewife; I have one younger brother. I played the violin and enjoyed family musical gatherings with my father who plays the accordion. I lived my life with the motto to *"find your calling"* and to stick to it because you should never quit. Since I had such a solid, resolute, responsible, strong, and supportive background, I can, it enables me to successfully solve problems. My life is full of blessings, weaved by my love of work, marriage, and wonderful 4 children and 4 grandchildren. This gives me the strength and joy to share my blessings with others.

As I finished my schooling, I had a need to discover my passion for science and a healthy lifestyle. I wanted to learn everything I could about health. My dad and I became vegans when I was fifteen years old. My mom had a hard time adapting to a healthy lifestyle. She struggled with dietary changes and endured thyroid problems throughout her life. Her addictions to coffee and cigarettes eventually created her lung cancer. She never complained about her thyroid problems and the accompanying fatigue and ended up having surgery. Today, at the Hippocrates Health Institute, after seeing so many women and men with thyroid problems, I understand my mother so much better. The thyroid gland is your body regulator and balances the metaobolic function. She passed away in 2001 from lung cancer and she is so missed. Your mother is where you come from; she is *"larger than life"* for you. I still find myself picking up the phone, wanting to call her.

My dad is doing great in his late 80s: still as athletic as always and interested in learning new things. In so many ways, he's shown me how to live and how to handle responsibilities. We both believe that work is a part of life, not who we are.

My focus on medicine started with various courses on science and a range of university courses from biology to physics. My interest in medicine began in Sweden, where I directed the Brandal Clinic, a government-supported, natural, residential, healthcare center. When I emigrated to the United States in 1983, I concluded a full time nursing curriculum. I apprenticed during this transatlantic period, and my health care career was now in full swing and I never looked back.

Having settled in the United States, I joined the Hippocrates team in Boston. Education has always been of great interest to me, and soon drove me to earn my doctorate in nutritional science and become a naturopathic doctor. I am always learning and fortunate to have found a field that still interests me every day. For more than 30 years, I have led the Hippocrates Medical team as a lead health administrator. This has been one of the most rewarding experiences in my life. I have authored or co-authored six books on progressive human health.

My work affords ongoing opportunities to conduct global conferences and media interviews. The media suppresses so much of what a woman is, urging women to *"just stay young and pretty"* by poisoning ourselves with sweet fragrances loaded with chemicals that are placed on our bodies, in our clothes, etc., making us toxic. We become sexual objects, rather than the significant pillar of strength, power, kindness, and care that inherently personifies our gender.

As I continued on my journey in the health field, I travelled around the world with my husband, Dr. Brian Clement. I learned to recognize the eagerness for women to create a healthy family, and how balance, harmony, and fertility are totally dependent on healthy individuals within the family. In this time of technology, we have unfettered access to information about what is good or bad and can make our own decisions about lifestyle, diet, exercise, and relaxation. All the choices, however simple, seem to add to our confusion; we have a hard time making clear, instinctual decisions. The joy of the daily routines of exercise, hygiene, gratitude, and feeding your body real nourishment is supplanted by a pseudo-existence filled with stress, fueled by a processed diet, and fed by toxic medications that are supposed to keep us going.

The many women that I meet as I travel around the globe all seem to be concerned with creating a healthy family and balancing their work and family lives. The experience of talking with them has shown me their interest in confronting issues and has made it clear to me that women have much to offer regarding work experience. For example, one client, who is a medical doctor, attended HHI's three-week Life Transformation Program and confided in me about her lifestyle, sharing a viewpoint that I felt would be of interest to all. She was concerned about the balance of home and work. When I suggested that she answer the questionnaire that we posed to a group of leaders, she graciously accepted but chose to remain anonymous. Here, however, are her answers:

1. What axiom do you feel is the secret to your success, the most important mantra in keeping your leadership unique?

The secret of my success is to "do unto others as you would have them do unto you and your loved ones." This mantra has served me well as a physician and caregiver of patients from all walks of life, ethnicities, and socio-economic backgrounds.

2. What accomplishments are you most proud to have been part of, and how did you achieve these successes?

One major accomplishment took place right after graduating medical school. I cofounded a scholarship fund with my godmother, for undergraduate college students in my hometown. It was always our goal to "give back" to those less fortunate, to help them achieve academic success.

3. How would you describe your relationships with your closest colleagues, and with the people that you depended on to get the job done?

I have a positive and professional working relationship with my colleagues and coworkers. I believe in teamwork and encourage those around me to do the same. There is no possible way to provide the best medical care to patients without teamwork. Each of us has a different title and job description but in order to maximize success, we each must step outside of our respective roles and pitch in wherever needed.

4. How did you deal with stress and how did you handle conflicts with your team members?

I deal with stress by separating myself from the situation immediately and having a few brief minutes of quiet time—deep breathing and silent meditation. I prefer to handle conflict with team members, one on one, using a non-confrontational approach.

5. How would you describe your career stages, and what were the major turning points that helped you reach your highest level?

My career stages have evolved with my lifestyle, reflecting both my personal and family needs. The major turning point in my career, a change that restored balance to my life, was when my contract was not renewed at a rural health clinic. I believe it was due to financial reasons, but the love and compassion expressed upon my departure—not just by my patients but by the entire community—was overwhelming. Although we all regretted it at the time, it was a blessing in disguise! It allowed me the opportunity to seek employment closer to home with better hours, and freed up time to enable my direct participation in the care of my aging mother. I consider this the highest level of my achievement.

6. What inspired you and how did you inspire the people who worked with you? How did people help you accomplish your goals, and how did you help them accomplish theirs?

I get my inspiration from God and the many blessings that have been bestowed upon me. I stand on the shoulders of so many individuals who made sacrifices in their lives in order for me to have a better one: my parents, godmother, grandparents, mentors, and ancestors. It is my goal to make them proud by doing my best to contribute to the universe in a positive way.

7. What would you like to communicate about your leadership style, experience, or where you are now?

My leadership style is to encourage participation from all members of the team. I have found that open dialogue can uncover some of the brightest ideas from the individuals you least suspect.

Women are often portrayed as dainty and weak, even though we endure pain at many levels. Our emotions are heightened due to estrogen (which enhances discomfort) and stress (which frames and expands painful experiences). Additionally, our bodily burdens of noxious waste and acidity, intensify our discomfort neurologically. My four decades of experience—starting in Europe, and, since the 1980s at Hippocrates—has taught me that serene environments, bodily detoxi-fication, and authentic emotional work often permanently reduce or eliminate pain. Becoming women—the onset of menstruation—is often our first brush with the inner workings of our anatomy. Bearing children, menopause, emotional maternal obstacles, etc., all are unique to the feminine persona. All of these natural-occurring stages of life's normality can be embraced when we gracefully accept what a gift it is to be a powerful woman. We hold the keys to humanity's future.

We need to see the big picture if we wish to change our lives instead of only the details. Once we have the vision, then we can take the first baby steps toward finding our niche and being healthy. For example, I am now focusing my efforts on a project to educate women about using breathable, natural, chemical-free fabrics. Natural-fabric products, especially bras, are superior to synthetic clothing that suf-focates the skin, and they support the environment and greater health. I am dedicated to offering healthy options for young women to feel free and supported, literally and figuratively. We have a vision of a great future. We all want healthy lives.

Here are my responses to three of the questions we asked: How would you describe your relationship with your closest colleagues and people that you depended on to get the job done?

I listen intently to my clients to understand their situations and help them figure the best solutions for them. The people I work with are part of our team and I remain positive with all of them and do not play favorites. We cannot change people; therefore, we need to accept their strengths and weaknesses and work together in harmony. I am open to suggestions and respond to all who ask my opinion or help. Our colleagues respect each other.

How did you deal with stress and how did you handle conflicts with your team members?

I share my experiences and opinions with others and if there are conflicts, I listen to both sides and remain open to solutions. I remind everyone we are a team and to keep tolerance as our main objective so that we can serve others. I deal with stress by following my eight hour mantra: eight hours of sleep, eight hours of play, and eight hours of work. I enjoy exercise and keep balanced by being aware of what is missing from my routine. I love to laugh and laughter releases stress and is a great benefit to healthy living.

How would you describe your career stages, and what were the major turning points that helped you reach your highest level?

My life has been devoted to helping others get to a better place in their lives. I can only share what I know and be there for others to discuss their concerns. I offer suggestions and many women are concerned with balance, harmony and well-being. I believe that well-being is totally dependent on strong female leadership and if you do not take care of yourself you cannot take care of others. My turning point was making the decision to come to the United States, and then of course to be Brian's partner (at work and home), and mother to four amazing children. We have been fortunate to have a great partnership that is synergetic and our energy helps others find their energy. I am now mentoring others to pass on my knowledge since this is the ultimate stage of sharing. I am extremely happy being a mother, grandmother and wife. This is my balance.

References

Amen, D. *Healing ADD: The Break Through Program That Allows You to See and Heal the 6 Types of ADD*. Penguin Group, New York, NY, 2001.

Bandura, A. *Social Foundations of Thought and Action: A Social Cognitive Theory*. Prentice Hall, Englewood Cliffs, NJ, 1986.

Bandura, A. *Self-Efficacy: The Exercise of Control*. W. H. Freeman, New York, NY, 1997.

Buckley, V. *Christina Queen of Sweden: The Restless Life of a European Eccentric*. Harper Perennial, London, UK, 2004.

Carson, R. *The Sea Around Us*. Oxford University Press, New York, NY, 1951.

Chopra, D. & Tanzi R. *Super Brain: Unleashing the Explosive Power of Your Mind to Maximize Health, Happiness, and Spiritual Well-Being*. Harmony Books, New York, NY, 2013.

Cooper, J. C. *Taoism: The Way of the Mystic*. Harper Collins, New York, NY, 1990.

Clement, A. M. & Clement B.R. *Killer Clothes*. Book Pub Co., Summertown, TN, 2011.

Clement, B. R. & Clement A. M. *7 Keys to Lifelong Sexual Vitality*. New World Library, Novato, CA, 2012.

Clement, B. R. & Powell, K.C. *Belief: Integrity in Relationships*. Hippocrates Health Institute, West Palm Beach, FL, 2013.

Clinton, H. *It Takes a Village*. Simon & Schuster, New York, NY, 2006.

Cloud, H. & Townsend, J. *Boundaries: When to Say Yes, How to Say No To Take Control of Your Life*. Zondervan, Grand Rapids, MI, 1992.

Connell, R. *Gender*. Polity Press, Oxford, UK, 2002.

Craig, G.J. *Human Development: An Integrated Study of Life Span*. Prentice Hall, Upper Saddle River, NJ, 1994.

De Beauvoir, S. *The Second Sex*. Knopf Doubleday Pub Group, New York, NY, 1949.

Durant, W. *The Story of Philosophy: the Lives and Opinions of the Greater Philosophers*. Washington Square Press, New York, NY, 1961.

Erikson, E. *Childhood and Society*. Norton & Co, New York, NY, 1963.

Erikson, E. & Erikson, J. *The Life Cycle Completed*. Norton & Co, New York, NY, 1987.

Feist, J. & Feist, G.J. *Theories of Personality*. McGraw-Hill, Boston, MA, 2002.

Freud, S. *The Interpretation of Dreams*. HarperCollins Publishers, New York, NY, 1900.

Friedan, B. *The Feminine Mystique*. Dell Pub, Co., New York, NY, 1963.

Fuller, M. *Woman in the Nineteenth Century*. Dover Pub, Canada, 1999.

Gardner, H. *Intelligences Reframed: Multiple Intelligences for the 21st century*. Basic Books, New York, NY 1999.

Gilligan, C. *In a Different Voice: Psychological Theory and Women's Development*. Harvard University Press, Cambridge, MA, 1982.

Goleman, D., Kaufman, P., & Ray, M. *The Creative Spirit*. Plume Books, New York, NY, 1993.

Goleman, D. *Emotional Intelligence*. Bantam Books, New York, NY, 1995.

Golombok, S. & Fivush, R. *Gender Development*. Cambridge University Press, New York, NY, 1994

Goodall, J. *Reason for Hope: A Spiritual Journey*. Grand Central Publishing, New York, NY, 1999.

Hall, J.A. *Nonverbal Sex Differences: Accuracy of Communication and Expressive Style*. John Hopkins University Press, Baltimore, MD, 1984.

Horney, K. *Feminine Psychology*. Norton & Co, New York, NY, 1967.

Horney, K. *The Neurotic Personality of Our Time*. Norton & Co. New York, NY, 1964.

Jacobs C. & Wendel I. *The Everything Parents Guide to ADHD in Children*. Adams Media, Avon, MA, 2010.

Maslow, A.H. *Motivation and Personality*. Viking Press, New York, NY, 1954.

Mead, M. *Male and Female: The Classic Study of the Sexes:* William Morrow & Co., New York, NY, 1967.

Miller, A. *The Drama of the Gifted Child: The Search for the True Self*. Harper Collins, New York, NY, 1981.

Miller, J. B. *Toward a New Psychology of Women*. Beacon Press, Boston, MA, 1986.

Ormrod, J. E. *Educational Psychology: Developing Learners*. Prentice Hall, Saddle River, NJ, 2003.

Perl, E. *Mating in Captivity: Unlocking Erotic Intelligence*. Harper Perennial, New York, NY, 2009.

Pirie, M. *100 Great Philosophers: Makers of Modern Thought*. MFJ Books, New York, NY, 2009.

Powell, K. C. *Developmental Psychology of Adolescent Girls: Conflicts and Identity Issues*. Education Journal, 125 (1), pgs. 77–96, 2004.

Powell, K. C. *Educational Psychology of the Self: An Inter-Active Workbook.* Kendall Hunt, Dubuque, IA, 2006.

Powell, K. C. *Educational Psychology of the Self and Learning.* Pearson, Boston, MA, 2012.

Randolph, C. W. & James, G. *From Hormone Hell to Hormone Well.* Health Communications, Inc. Deerfield Beach, FL, 2009.

Sandberg, S. *Lean In: Women, Work and the Will to Lead.* Knopf Double Day Pub Group, New York, NY, 2013.

Santrock, J. W. *Educational Psychology.* McGraw-Hill, Boston, MA, 2012.

Shoknoff, J. P. *Protecting Brains, Not Simply Stimulating Minds.* Science. 333(6045), pp. 982–983, 2011.

Skinner, B.F. *About Behaviorism,* Alfred A. Knopf, New York, NY, 1974.

Slavin, R.E. *Cooperative Learning: Theory, Research, and Practice.* Allyn & Bacon, Boston, MA, 1995.

Spar, D. L. *Wonder Woman: Sex Power and the Conquest for Perfection.* Sarah Crichton Books, New York, NY, 2014

Stein, M. *Jung's Map of the Soul: An Introduction.* Open Court Publishing, Chicago, IL, 1998.

Sternberg, R. *Metaphors of Mind: Conceptions of the Nature of Intelligence.* Cambridge University Press, New York, NY, 1990.

Storr, A. *The Essential Jung.* MJF Books, New York, NY, 1983.

Tannen, D. *Gender and Discourse.* Oxford University Press, New York, NY, 1994.

Tannen, D. *Talking from 9 to 5.* William Morrow & Co., New York, NY, 1994.

Tyson, P. & Tyson, R.M. *Psychoanalytic Theories of Development: An Integration.* Yale University Press, New Haven, CT, 2009.

Vaknin, S. *Malignant Self-Love: Narcissism Revisited.* A Narcissus Publications, Skopje Macedonia, 2003.

Vygotsky, D. & Christie, J. *Thought and Language.* MIT Press, Cambridge, MA, 2009.

Vygotsky, L.S. *Mind in society: The Development of Psychological Processes.* Harvard University Press, Cambridge, MA, 1978.

Warren, E. *A Fighting Chance.* Metropolitan Books, New York, NY, 2014.

Welstead, S. *Searching for You: Ideas About Healthy Relationships.* Volumes Pub, Canada, 2009.

Wheatley, M. *Turning to One Another: Simple Conversations to Restore Hope in the Future.* Berrett-Koehler Publishers, San Francisco, CA, 2002.

Wollstonecraft, M. *A Vindication of the Rights of Women.* Courier Dover Pub, Mineola, NY, 1792.

Woolfolk, A. *Educational Psychology.* Allyn & Bacon, Boston, MA, 2011.

Wikipedia & Google provided URLs for names, dates, and other information.

The Balance of Power

The Power of Balance